THE GENESIS OF FALCON

I0618736

THE GENESIS OF FALCON

SPM Publications

London

SPM Publications, Unit 136, 113-115 George Lane,
South Woodford, London E18 1AB

www.spmpublications.com

First published in Great Britain by SPM Publications – an imprint of
Sentinel Writing & Publishing Company Ltd in November 2013

ISBN 978-0-9927055-2-7

Set in Palatino Linotype

Appreciation

The Genesis of Falcon is an anthology of the winning, commended and specially mentioned poems and stories from the Sentinel Annual Poetry and Short Story Competitions 2012 judged by Roger Elkin and David Caddy.

The themes, styles and skills in the poems and stories compiled in this book are as varied as they are exciting. They explore everyday situations in life weaving in the complexities and the simplicities, the joys and the pains, in ways that will have you in parts laughing out loud, smiling and chuckling in other parts and shedding a tear in others. I really congratulate the authors included in this book for the achievement.

All of us at Sentinel Writing & Publishing Company offer special thanks to the hundreds of writers from across the world that have supported our writing competitions over the years. In the present global economic climate, writers are choosing carefully the competitions they enter, and some writers at this time would not give a pay-to-enter competition the time of day. Our competitions are not supported by any government or other grants, therefore they are funded primarily from the entry fees, and our own funds. It is a privilege to have so many writers believe in us this way and keep faith with us.

Our judges have also been amazing. Roger Elkin has now judged our annual poetry competition three times while David Caddy has just judged our first annual short story competition. They have done a great job and I am proud to compile in this anthology the selections made by these esteemed writers in their own right.

Happy Reading

Nnorom Azuonye
Publishing Director, SPM Publications

CONTENTS

Poems

Short Stories

STEVE SCHOLEY

The Harmony of Swallows

Wrist-thick, with whipped and knotted end,
the rope hangs in irresistible invitation
beneath the pan-tiles of the campanile
of St. Nicolas. Open-sided, oaken,
the heavy frame stands alone, closer to tavern
than to chapel. You jump, grip, pull,
and seven years of child's weight dangles,
closer to Earth than to the vaults of Heaven,
framed beneath the dull and cobwebbed bell.
Within its upturned bowl, your body could have curled,
serene in rest or sleep. Again, you leap; and this time,
having learned, assessed the angles, take a run:
your small weight curves and the clapper slaps the lip.
Once tongued, the bronze bell clangs, resonant,
the peal appalling in the calm;
twice, it clangs again, reverberates
around the wooded vale. Alarmed
by the elements of its tune – the throbbing hum,
the strike tone, tierce and quint, the piercing nominal –
you pitch, diminuendo, run to my arms.
Fledgling swallows in their nest above sit unperturbed.

LESLEY BURT

Freeze-framed

Your dad squints into
the box Brownie and says: stand still.
You are in front of knee-high stumps,
bent over the cricket bat
waiting for your mum
to bowl underarm.

You wear a smile beneath
a hair-ribbon and Kirby-grip;
the breeze holds the hem of your dress;
your brother cups his hands,
poised to run as soon as
you thwack the tennis-ball.

There you all are in black and white,
thinking of nothing further ahead
than a flask of tea and ham sandwiches.

JOHN ROBINSON

To My Wife, Our Life.

Conversation ended for you and me in nineteen ninety-three,
when our communication degraded into snatches of chats
about neighbours, absent children and half-dead offerings
the cat brought in; and shopping lists and what to have for tea,
more specifically, what frozen treats we could thaw and eat.
And let's not forget the endless cycle of decorating,
between holiday trips to strips of sun-drenched beaches,
parboiling in our own sweat for eight hours a day
before spotting TV soap stars slipping into exotic bars,
as we crawled back to our all-inclusive holiday complex,
rammed with local themed gala nights and watery drinks.
And did we stop to think? No. For politics and the economy,
famine in Africa and that tsunami in the oriental east
we had the TV news, which we heard but mostly ignored,
unless someone famous was dead, or drowning
in a juicy scandal; then we listened to what was said.
And if someone we liked, asked earnestly for our money,
to save a child, or someone's sight, we agreed it was right
and that someone should do something about it.
Which we did; we gave gifts of goats on all our friends' behalves
and sent them notes to thank them for their generosity.
Then we discovered outlet stores and became sophisticated,
wearing famous names to frame our unique personalities,
while saving money, because of the flaws, you could hardly see.
We became an organic machine, running green and clean
from the safety of our sofa, and guided by the fickle plans
in glossy magazines, adopted many different lifestyle schemes.
None of which turned us towards each other, just around and out
towards the world, somehow hollowed out and hoping
that our inevitable dementia, is a trendy kind the papers follow.

EILIDH THOMAS

Sweet Wood and Apple Pie

In the land where the sweet cinnamon tree grows, the giant
cinnamon bird builds its cinnamon nest at the top of the
cinnamon tree.

quarter, core, peel and slice the apples – thick

It is said that at the funeral for his wife Poppaea Sabina,
Nero burned on her pyre a year's worth of the sweet wood of
cinnamon.

*beat butter and sugar for pastry with a whole egg and extra yolk (keep
the white for glazing later)*

Downwind from the shores of Ceylon the smell of cinnamon
drifts eight leagues out to sea.

*work in the flour and finish gathering the pastry together with your
hands – wrap and chill*

In his writings Pliny the Elder says that 350 grams of cinnamon
are worth 5,000 grams of silver.

mix sugar, cinnamon and some flour with the apples

Seductively, Cleopatra's spices were carried with her jewels.

*lightly roll and line a pie dish with pastry, pile the apples high, lattice
or cover with a lid of pastry and seal*

Cinnamon scents her garments like the smell of Lebanon. – Song
of Solomon

brush with egg white, sprinkle with caster sugar and bake until golden

I have perfumed my bed with myrrh, aloes, and cinnamon. –
Proverbs 7:17

cool slightly from the oven and sprinkle with sugar

From the magic fire of cinnamon, myrrh and spikenard the
Phoenix rises from the ashes.

serve warm with softly whipped cream

DEBORAH HARVEY

An Approximation

> *'Sauntering along,*
> *the boy looks up and sees a tree filled with angels,*
> *bright angelic wings bespangling every bough like stars'*
>   *from 'The Life of William Blake' by Alexander Gilchrist*

Oh, there've been hints, intimations.
Cumbrous rustlings in twigs. A silvery
glister that might have been
more substantial than moonlight.

I've noticed drifts of feathers falling
from viridian fan-vaulting,
heard gears creak
as flight machinery unfurls.

One morning
while I was out walking,
I heard a lime at the roadside singing
It's a beautiful day.

OK, it wasn't the tree.
It wasn't an airy deity either
just dangling legs in scruffy jeans
and unlaced trainers.

I don't suppose I'll ever witness an oak
list under a cargo of seraphim
yet late autumn days, out on the Levels
mistletoed trees in orchards

flutter star-scattered wings,
and as countless cacophonous voices fly
I might dream an approximation of angels
          on Peckham Rye.

CATHERINE EDMUNDS

Later

he trundles his bicycle into the light
through grains of silence
past four men walking the ploughed fields
in search of windmills

at home
his face wears a frown
and the piping along the edge of his dressing gown
flirts with moths

his wife left him yesterday
or maybe last year
or even some previous decade, with flowers and hair
blowing this way and that

and the streams run into the ground
beneath the grey pterodactyls –
or that's what he thinks he sees through his cataracts
'get them done,' she used to say
but he never did as he was told:
that's why his front forks are buckled; he won't
be able to cycle again

there's a frog on a rock in his garden
it glistens

he doesn't even know it's there
he doesn't remember the way to the pond
he's forgotten about newts and water boatmen

his bicycle's broken
that's all he knows, that's all that matters
she's not coming back

JOHN LINDLEY

John 'Hangman' Ellis

With thirty years of trapdoor and drop
to his name, John Ellis divided his throat
(ironic or what?) with a clean sweep;
turned to the razor when life's knot

got too tight. Not for him chair, rope
and the dead man's dance. Not for him
the wrench, sway and dangle. The quick rip
was good enough to quit life's grim

joke. John Ellis, spur of the moment, saw
no time for reflection or final note,
lost it in that moment – barbershop floor
to his cheekbone, red reservoir at his throat.

'Barber'. Let's not forget that. 'Barber'.
So maybe that cut-throat was apt after all.
The hanging and roadshow years over,
hearing his and the Nation's depression call.

Did it ever occur to him before,
I wonder, when lathering that blade
on a leather strap? Who knows for sure
how such impossible choices get made:

asp or gas, whisky and pills, arsenic
or Lysol, train track, river or pond
and – my God! All those slick blade and bullet-
in-the-mouth bargains with the beyond?

LINDA BURNETT

Stand-off with hare

I look again: its eye is staring gold,
but poised with the delicacy of moths,
about to discharge impulsively in startled flight.
It is so old – the look, that is – imperious, bold,
centred with tunnel-black, reaching from the pit
of its brain, as if shot through with piercing insight
or superior sensibility. Pure instinct so finely pitched
the merest whisper ruffling one ear tip
transmits thrills of muscle down to its feet,
like the undulating flaps of shaken table cloth.

I am exposed; insouciant, the hare stands firm,
the means of quick escape confident in its limbs,
its face marsupial, as though theatrically posed
for camera lens. The haughty pout, a slight upturn
angled to catch the most fetching light,
orchestrates breath for both of us: the hare's composed;
mine barely supporting life for that short spell.
We square up at our O.K. Corral:
fixed amber beads blaze none of my stage fright,
but see beyond me, waiting on a whim.

It cannot last. The starkness of its gaze dissolves
my bones, yet flashes an imperative to hold.
The ecstasy of stillness shrinks away,
rehearsing how the stand-off might be solved.
Neither will yield an inch to make a move,
locked as we are in our all-consuming play.
The hare's form jerks with epileptic jolt –
the untested threat more pressing than my own.
Its brusque dismissal feels intended to reprove;
I stand bereft, and now unutterably cold.

OZ HARDWICK

The Genesis of Falcon

By the time He had done chickens,
puffins, parrots, and everything else
He hadn't got round to naming,
He had the measure of creation
with His eyes shut: Health & Safety
had flown out of the window.

Cocky and careless, He scrabbled flight
into hard lines, stabbed neat feathers
into a frame stripped bare to electric flex,
soldered eyes like beacons flashing
warnings of height and death.

Perfection came easy: Bird rebooted
to ripping machine of beak and talons
gripping His wrist. He held it close,
kissed his creation, inspired it with steel,
darkness and plunging fire.

Blood Dress – For Maya and Daisy
RHUAR DEAN

1.

"The designer is Israeli, but he lives in Berlin. These dresses are exclusive to our outlet here in Stockholm."

"It's beautiful isn't it?" Cassie opened the trail of the dress. "Look at its shape, it cuts into the chest and the trail it's just, it's just," she paused looking down at the dress. "It's just an explosion, of form, colour. It's so perfect. The crimps in the material match the cut, it's totally bizarre. Look at the way it juts down off the shoulder and then, just as it draws in at the waist, the colour bursts into something almost floral, but then almost like a kaleidoscope, or like that scene in 2001 A Space Odyssey when he falls through the star-gate. It's natural. But then industrial as well. And the trail, oh, it is just *meant* to be."

"It is very striking." Her husband leant back, arms folded, trying to dig into the instinct that had spurred Cassie's excitement.

"Would you like to try it on?" the shopkeeper asked. Cassie turned away and looked out of the window.

"I think she must," her husband said.

"Yes, you're right, of course. I must."

She looked at once seductive and innocent. Standing in front of the mirror she tried her various guises. A casual drop of the shoulder and tilt of the head exposed her neck in a way that would draw the men in a room to want to stoop and to kiss. A straightening of her pose, standing square to the mirror and she became suddenly chic, intimidating. Each man in the room would question whether he was dressed well enough to speak to her. Her husband and the shop assistant looked on, giving her space to make believe, both equally pleased to be allowed the show.

"Oh my god, it's so fucking perfect." Cassie's pose transformed into that of an excited schoolgirl as she threw her arms out at either side and stamped her feet in a dancing motion. No matter what she did the dress crimped and changed with her, taking on her mood, dancing with her excitement. She bent down at the knees and was still, gazing up to the mirror. She bit her lip in an attempt to cut some reality back into the freight train that had exploded in her chest.

"How much is it?" she clenched her fists hard at either side, standing rigid like a stubborn child.

The shopkeeper smiled, but before she could answer a man's body broke, shoulder first, through the shop window. All three flung themselves away as a shower of glass peppered the room. Cassie fell headlong into a rack of dresses that crumpled around her.

Stunned, they looked up from the floor at the jagged remains of the top half of the window that cut down above the man, who lay still in the centre of the display. A long crack ran up from the ridge of open air to the top of the frame like a jut of fork lightening above a mountain range. They searched for strings to reconnect their thoughts to the world as a thinner crack worked its way upwards along an invisible fault line, winding quicker each time the breeze picked up. In a few seconds it had worked its way to the larger crack at the centre, where it stopped. They held their breath and, at the first spark of relief, a chunk of glass, the size of a toaster, clicked free. It landed clean in the man's side and wedged rigid, oscillating gently after impact.

At this point the world rushed in. A whirl of screaming in the street hurried their return. The shopkeeper jumped up, shouting about helping the man. Cassie's husband was just behind. The two of them took him by his wrists and dragged him into the shop and away from the hanging glass in the window frame. A long trail of red dropped down from the window ledge behind him as he flopped to the floor. Blood pulsed from his neck and from one of his forearms. A long gash ran down from his forehead, through his eye socket and across his nose, the tip of which was missing.

"Call an ambulance," Cassie shouted to the shopkeeper as she gathered up a small pile of dresses and worked with her husband to put pressure on the man's wounds. A policeman arrived within minutes and then the paramedics. Cassie and her husband stepped out of the shop, both covered in blood. Soon after the man was gone, whisked away on a stretcher through a crowd of tourists to a waiting ambulance on the road.

A paramedic came to check them over but they weren't hurt. They were ushered back into the shop where they gave statements to the police. There was no explanation as to why, or even what, had caused him to come through the window. Once she had given her statement Cassie turned to look at herself in the mirror. The dress still hung just as beautifully from her shoulders, only now a dark streak of blood cascaded down from her right breast to the colour at her waist and the hem of the skirt was rimmed in a thin strip of darkness, just above her ankles. The train was limp and heavy, sodden through.

The shopkeeper came over. "Now that you have given your statement I must ask you to leave. The owner is on her way and once the police are finished we will need to get some specialist cleaners into the shop and talk to the insurers. Obviously we will be closed for a few days."
"I must have it," Cassie was still looking at herself in the mirror.
"I'm sorry, but it's the only one we have in this style."
"That's OK, I want this one."
"But all of the blood? It is ruined for certain."
"I don't care. I must have it. I want this one."
"Honey, surely not – it's covered in blood?"
"It's perfect. Only now is it *really* perfect."
"I'm sorry, but I couldn't possibly give you this one. If you give me your details I can see if we have anything similar in stock and perhaps we can send you one. Or you could come back in a few days. How long will you be in Stockholm?" She looked at Cassie's husband pleadingly.

"No." Cassie turned to face them, her body shrunk, diminutive. "No, I must have this one. I will pay for it, I - I don't mind paying for it. I'm not asking you to give it to me for free."

"Honey, really? Come on, you're in shock. Surely you don't mean that."

"I do."

"Impossible. I cannot," the shopkeeper huffed loudly. "There is just no way I can sell you that dress. Please," she indicated the changing room at the back of the store. "Please, if you don't mind. You must change back into your own clothes and leave the dress here. I have a lot to do now to get this place in order. It's a mess and I don't have time to stand here and argue, so, please. Get changed."

"If you won't sell it to me then I will turn around and walk out of the shop without paying for it. You can come after me if you like, or ask the police to arrest me. I don't care. I'm not taking it off."

The woman huffed again and hunched her shoulders, hands on her hips and staring quizzically at Cassie. Her face lightened and she nodded. "Listen, why don't you take it back to your hotel for now. I understand if you don't want to change yet. Where are you staying?"

"The Hilton," her husband replied.

"OK. Take it for now and I will come and pick it up later this evening, when you've calmed down."

2.

"I'm not going to give it back," Cassie hadn't moved from the mirror beside the wardrobe door since they arrived back at the hotel. Her husband sat showered on the bed in a dressing gown, perplexed and wandering what to do as he dried his hair with a towel.

"Cassie, if you don't calm down soon I'm gonna call a doctor. You're acting crazy and I think you're in shock."

"I'm not in shock," she ran her hand along the lip of the neckline, down the front, pulling slightly at the fabric. "I mean, it was shocking, yes. And I was shocked, yes. But I'm not *in* shock."

"What about the floor, there's blood on the carpet? Why don't you just head into the bathroom and take it off in there. We can hang it up then and work out what to do next, after you've had a shower."

"Have you ever seen anything like that, Adrian? Have you ever seen anyone as broken?" She bit her lip.

"No, never. Never so close. It was horrible, and I'm almost certain he's dead."

"Why are you so certain?"

"Look, you've got blood all along your legs," he pointed with his towel. "Why don't you have a shower honey?"

"Why are you so certain he's dead?"

"Because he lost *a lot* of blood, and he wasn't moving at all, and. We'll I don't know for sure."

"Exactly, you don't know for sure."

Her husband stood up and walked over to her, placing his hands on her shoulders. "Come on honey, really, we need to get you in the shower." He tried to turn her towards the bathroom but she resisted, placing her hand on his.

"There's a part of him here, on this dress. Do you think his wife or his girlfriend would want it? Do you think they would wear it?"

"Listen honey, if you don't calm down soon and stop acting crazy then I'm calling a doctor for sure."

She touched a finger to her breast and lifted it up in front of her. It blushed with the man's blood on its imprint. Slowly she placed it into her mouth, and closed her lips tight around it, sucking hard and closing her eyes.

"Right, that's enough," her husband took her by the shoulders and spun her around to face him, wrenching her hand from her mouth. She opened her eyes in shock.

"Fuck you," she shouted and tried to wriggle free but he forced her backwards, down onto the bed.

"Fuck you, fuck you, fuck you," she screamed, thrashing her body about but he held her flat against the bed. Eventually she settled, breathing heavily.

"Look," she was gazing up at her finger. "Look what you did." A thin trickle of blood ran down from her finger to her wrist where it had been cut by her teeth as he pulled it from her mouth. "That's my blood, not his." Her chest heaved beneath him as she fixed her stare on the blood. Her husband lay with his body across hers, his head to its side against her shoulder and hands pinning her back at the elbows.

"I'm sorry." He jumped up and pulled her by her wrist into a standing position. "Come on we've got to clean that hand right now." He tried to pull her towards the bathroom but she swung her free hand in an arc, crashing it into his face across the bridge of his nose and causing him to fall backwards onto the bed. As he fell he pulled her down on top of him. She knelt up and shoved her hand into the blood that had begun to run down over his mouth and chin.

"There, now you're bleeding as well," he pushed her away half-heartedly. She stood up on the bed and turned to face herself in the mirror, wiping her bloodied hand down from her breast, along a similar path to the bloodstain.

"Look at it now," she stood fixated with herself in the mirror. "The blood dress."

The End

Top Table Invitation
STEPHEN ATKINSON

He ceased to struggle the instant he sobered to the realization that if the immense winged creature above him actually let go he would plummet thousands of feet to certain doom among the grim, forbidding mountain peaks below.

It was black and vulture-like, like a condor, but more than twice the size of any he had ever seen in the Andes. Its talons were as big and powerful as anvils and his near naked body hung like a rag doll crumpled and awkward in their clutch. His desperate efforts to escape had left his entire length flayed and striped with blood-red wheals, but his groin and his waist where the giant talons gripped were worst. His back too felt as if it were about to snap. The bitter, high-altitude winds thundered in his ears yet, absurdly, his IPod still clung to his neck and dangled precariously below him, one earpiece close enough to emit the tinny thrust of Tchaikovsky's Cossack Dance.

"Don't be so damned arrogant, John!" Georgina was losing it big time, but then she always let people get under her skin, especially John. To his credit, his feathers remained unruffled, only Matt and Josie broadcast alarm bell signals to each other with one fleeting but knowing glance. Matt grimaced into his glass of Sauvignon.

With an exasperated grunt somewhere between a sigh and suicide, Georgina smacked her own forehead with the palm of her hand.

"God, you really are the most smug, complacent bastard I have ever met."

John raised his glass to toast his own wickedness. "Blame yourself, darling," he grinned devilishly. "You have given me every single thing I have ever wanted. Where else was there for me to go but to the land of smug complacency?"

The giant bird swept down onto a small rocky plateau just a few feet across and dumped John's broken body on the edge of a drop deep enough to stack dozens of Empire States. It stood beside him, towering at more than man height as it preened its wings. He lay uncomfortably on the ground watching it carefully. The behemoth knew its prey was secure, there was no chance of escape; except down to certain death.

John inspected the giant talons, stained with his own blood, and knew the truth. The bird could have killed him at any time – one tiny squeeze and he would have been history, Man-Jam. The monster was keeping him alive on purpose; he wanted his meat fresh. John peered over the edge of the precipice and felt dizzy with vertigo. He struggled to his feet and had to whip up his hands to his face as the bird stopped his preening and lunged his foot-long beak at his eyes.

"Jesus, you're trying to blind me," he shouted out loud, but he was also aware it was deliberately keeping its strength in check for fear of spilling its dinner over the edge.

Nonetheless, time and time again the beak lunged at him and his hands were stripped of folds of flesh as he sought to protect himself. He dropped to his knees to hide his eyes from the creature and only then did the assault stop. John peered through his bloodied fingers at the sight before him; a brilliant blue sky with other winged creatures soaring nearby, some perhaps as large as this one who was keeping him jealously guarded for himself. He was only aware of one emotion stronger than the pain that wracked his entire body from head to toe; fear. Fear of what was going to happen next. The two watched each other suspiciously, yet John could detect a confidence in the other's eyes, a cocky confidence he himself could not possibly muster.

Matt coughed gently. "I think, to be fair Georgina, all John was saying was that as we are pretty much at the top of the food chain then we should at least be grateful."

"I think, to be fair Matthew," mocked Georgie in a comical falsetto. "All John was saying was that any vegetarian is a lily-livered liberal who deserves to be gobbled up by the first thing on four legs to call him Dinner."

John laughed and with palpable relief Matt and Josie downgraded the alert to Amber.

"I've heard Victorian women actually hoped they would find themselves pretty hosts to a tapeworm, to keep them eternally slim," he rejoined.

"Oh my God," exclaimed Josie, her face suddenly shock-white and clasping her open, slack mouth with her hands. "How would you ever be rid of it?"

Matt joined in the fun. "Don't be daft, woman – when it had done its job it slithered off down to the nearest Burger King for a decent meal."

"You veggies are just like that," persisted John, his cruel streak running away with him. "Your sweet-n'-lows and rabbit food, low-calorie lettuce lunches are your modern-day tapeworms."

"Ugh!" Josie exclaimed, disgusted, pushing the last of the celery to the centre of the table.

"It is the natural order of things for man to eat meat. We are predators, just as we are intended to be, and there is no place for all your guilty weeping and wailing." John paused. "Besides, I like a big juicy tenderloin."

"You might feel differently if you were swimming around at the bottom of the food-chain pond," Josie chimed in more to offer Georgie some feminine back-up than to rekindle the argument.

"A sprat instead of a prat,"whispered Georgie in a snide sotto voce.

"Nonsense," replied John, leading with his chin. "I simply respect the intended order of things. As a sprat I would go willingly to the shark's table."

Georgie knew instantly she had him. Vicious victory shone in her eyes like neon napalm.

"Ah...so you're telling us that if a big hungry lion stumbled upon you without your equalising fire-stick you would lie down with your paws in the air and say 'Bon appetite, Leo, I think I would recommend me medium to well done, but I guess you'll be having me rare.' I don't think so." Georgie looked at Josie with a satisfying 'get-out-of-that' gleam. Even Matt raised an appreciative eyebrow as the sisters high-fived.

But John wasn't beaten yet. "Leo may be big but he's wrong if he thinks he's higher up the food chain than me," he responded. "I'd simply enlighten him that the female of the species is far, far tastier and offer up your address on his menu. With various recommended sauces etc etc... "

Luckily there was nothing heavier than an unwanted bread roll left on the table for Georgina to throw at him and it bounced off harmlessly as Matt and John staged their own gleeful high-five.

The next day Matt drove the girls into the nearest town for the markets while John poured himself into his £100 Calvin Klein swimming shorts for a serious tan session by the pool. It was hot and it was peaceful and he had enjoyed his huge sausage and bacon breakfast which loomed menacingly over Georgina's yoghurt and banana. Even Matt baulked at the Black Pudding.

"It'll put hairs on your chest," John had taunted him. "If they can find a landing strip wide enough to take root, that is."

He turned over for the umpteenth time onto his stomach, his IPod earphones exploding with the 1812 and his imagination grappling with his latest Murakami. He could feel the soothing caress of sunshine on his back and his calves, as intimate as any lover's touch. It was February and the Bolivian high summer sun still burned fiercely in the sky, trying to melt him into his plastic sunbed. Their borrowed villa was high in the mountains a long way from the claustrophobic chaos of La Paz. He was totally alone with the cicadas and the humming birds and his rum punch, mixed just the way he liked it.

He shivered, a little bad tempered, as something big blocked out the sun for a moment or two accompanied by a deep chill that sank deep into his soul.

He screamed in pain beyond any torture he had ever suffered as the creature once more sunk its talons into his midriff and took to the skies again. The bird answered with a decibel-busting cry of its own – an unholy squawk not of terror, but of triumph. John's eardrums all but burst and he tore the remains of the IPod leads from his head and threw them back into the empty skies below him. He stared at the bones in his fingers showing through the blood where the creature had virtually skinned him with its beak. He felt sick. Somehow he managed to turn his head and retched into the void beneath. Then mercifully he blacked out.

He awoke to find himself dumped unceremoniously on another cramped plateau, this one supporting a prickly nest containing three of the creature's young. The chicks were themselves almost man height and squawked and screeched with delight over their drop-in dinner.

Interwoven branches scratched and scraped his already battered body as he tried to hunker away to the very edge. But there was only one escape – and first he had to scale the thick trunks under the watchful eyes of the creature and its hungry brood. Several times he screamed in pain as beaks pecked deep into his back but desperately he kept going. How he wished he had simply jumped off into the abyss at their first stopping off point. Nothing could be worse than this.

Miraculously he made it to the top and managed to withstand the merciless barrage to fall gratefully off the side to the blue unknown beneath. He even managed a grim smile as his momentum gathered speed and he felt himself falling… falling… falling…

"Do you think we'll always be at the top of the food chain, I mean with evolution and all that?" Josie had asked innocently that previous evening.

John snorted and waved a dismissive hand to the heavens, even though the night was already deep and black. "That big sun up there is sitting around waiting for a good day to explode. The moon's drifting out of earth's orbit at something like half an inch every year. Whenever either of them goes, we go. Nothing lasts forever."

"Except your bloody penchant for pomposity," sneeredGeorgie under her breath.

As he plunged into unstoppable freefall, the grotesque squawking faded into the distance above him. But even as he tore through the endless nothingness beneath, he was convinced that at any moment he would awake to find himself in his soft bed with Georgie by his side. Too much red meat and too much red wine for dinner last night, that's all, he thought.

He always was a smug, complacent bastard.

The End

The Mysterious Man
DAVID CREWE

The tale, or at least the small part of it I am about to tell, was passed to me many years ago by a sailor I met whilst travelling among a group of islands far from the mainland off the eastern seaboard of south America. As I listened to his incredible story, words almost failed me. Now as I recall it, so does my ageing memory. You, dear reader, must make allowance for that.

I met the sailor in one of the many bawdy drinking houses next to the port on the largest of the group of islands. In those days, ships from around the world stopped there to trade goods, as well as stock up on provisions for the long voyages ahead. We had both been conducting business in the market and by chance had ended up in the same place in search of food and a bed for the night. I was immediately taken by his appearance for whilst he was a young man, he had something of the past about him, both in his features and his manner. There was also something quite ethereal about him, yet he was as much of flesh and blood as any man there.

He was tall and olive-skinned, with long dark hair and a powerful frame, and moved lightly on his feet. He wore a sword around his waist that reminded me of the portraits of buccaneers of years gone by, and yet it did not look at all out of place on him. I asked him about the sword to make conversation. He told me it had belonged to his father whom he hadn't known. Our conversation was slow to begin with, as he seemed uncomfortable talking to me. However, after we had been talking for some time, exchanging stories of our travels in far flung parts of the world he seemed to relax. Then, at my mentioning a storm I'd encountered some years before, the sailor appeared slightly startled and began to recount the story which I am about to pass on to you.

The tale he told me was of a mysterious man who had once arrived in a storm on an island not far from where we were. As to the timings of events I am unsure, all the sailor could tell me was that what happened had happened long before the time of my grandfather's grandfather. Of this he was sure. As he spoke however, I couldn't help but feel the events he recalled were not tales from generations past, but first hand recollections.

He bowed his head slightly and spoke quietly as he told me the following tale:

He arrived in the middle of the night in a small fishing town during the most ferocious storm ever witnessed by anybody still alive to tell tales. Those who had passed to the other side may well have witnessed worse, but of this we have no tales.

After the first three or four boats had failed to come back to shore, there began to form a general feeling of unease amongst the townspeople. Nothing was said, but nobody was immune to that sense of foreboding that spread silently from street to street and from house to house. When evening came and no boats had returned, fear proper started to set in, yet nobody ventured to the waterfront. Nobody set a beacon. Nobody made any attempt to establish what had happened to a quarter of the men of the town who had left before the sun came up that morning and had not returned. It was as if nobody knew what to do.

At sunset an eerie chill developed in the air and the people of the town started to return to their homes to light fires and settle the animals in for the night. The children of the town were unusually quiet.

Shortly after the last resident had disappeared from the streets, a flock of seagulls flew silently into the town square, settled calmly on the ground and died.

Around an hour after the seagulls arrived, a distant sound could be heard, an ominous low pitched rumble which seemed to come from all directions and filled every inch of space. The waves began to grow and the tide exaggerated, moving far out from the beach exposing shoals of dead fish before racing back toward the shore and crashing high up on the beach.

Then the wind and rain came.

The winds blew with such power that people feared for their lives even inside their houses. Roofs were blown away and trees felled by the sheer force. The rains fell so hard that crops in the fields were completely destroyed in minutes. The townspeople, in a state of panic, fled their houses and assembled in the market hall. Nobody could say why they had gone there. Nobody spoke.

The market hall was the only building left unscathed by the storm. The storm raged for several hours with such intensity that the townspeople were unable to communicate because the noise was so great that words would have been lost before leaving the lips, and as it was the pressure and noise of the storm was such that the minds of all present were rendered useless until it abated, which it did in an instant at the stroke of midnight.

It took a while for the silence outside to register with the townspeople gathered in the market hall and when finally it did, they left as if guided by invisible forces and congregated in the town square, in the dark, amidst the bodies of the seagulls.

It was then that he arrived, walking slowly to the square from the beach, each footstep ringing with a low metallic crash like a deadened church bell echoing about the hills around the town. He was short and elderly looking and was dressed in a long black cloak and had eyes that seemed not of this world, appearing to those who dared look at them to be deep and empty.

When he reached the square, with a sudden fast whip of his left arm he blew up a wind that almost lifted people from their feet. When the wind had died, he commanded the seagulls to fly and they immediately took off in their hundreds, screaming and flapping amongst the crowd. Those who were quick enough covered their faces against the clawing and pecking. Those who were not suffered greatly from the birds' attacks and there was sheer panic in the square.

With a second whip of his left arm, the birds were quiet.

He walked slowly though the crowd, who dispersed around him, and approached the well in the centre of the square. He sat on the small wall around the well and looked slowly about the crowd, measuring each person with his empty eyes. After some minutes he spoke. His voice was quiet and weak like that of an old man, yet it carried undiminished through the crowd and reached the ears of everyone.

'I have travelled far and am in need of rest,' he almost whispered. 'I trust you will permit me to stay here awhile.'
With that he closed his eyes and remained motionless for several seconds, breathing slowly.
'I am hungry, and need to eat.' He said, this time slightly louder. 'Bring me what you have, and don't try to spare anything for I can see all.'

The townspeople remained silent and still, not knowing what to do, when suddenly without opening his eyes or moving his mouth, the man let out a low and blood-curdling yell, 'Go now! I am hungry and must eat.'

People ran in all directions to fetch what animals they could. Each scared to return, lest their offering angered the man, yet too terrified to run away. Slowly they began to arrive back at the square with hastily slaughtered chickens, pigs, goats and baskets of fruits, all of which were laid in front of the man. He neither opened his eyes, stirred, nor spoke.

Then with a sudden and violent backwards jerk of his head and a frantic chewing motion he appeared to devour the offerings. As he chewed, the animals and fruit withered, decayed and turned to dust in an instant. All that remained was a dark covering of dust where the piles of food had been.

He stopped suddenly, his head still back, and motioned for the crowd to draw nearer. This they did en masse as though hypnotised. He leant forward slightly, opened his empty eyes, and spoke. 'I am not satisfied.'

The sailor slowed his speech slightly at this point and his voice faltered as he repeated the words, 'I am not satisfied.'

I was desperate to know more, and implored him to continue but this was as much as the sailor seemed willing to tell me and, rising from the table, he begged my pardon to leave. I asked him to stay and continue, but he gave me such a cold and hollow look that I understood he would not be persuaded. I thanked him for the most enthralling story, and bade him farewell. As he left, I could barely stop myself throwing questions at him.

'What became of the sailors that night?' I asked, 'Were the boats ever found? And the people of the town, what happened to them?'

He turned slowly and replied calmly but sadly, 'That will have to wait for another day my friend.'

I wanted to ask more but he silenced me with a wave of his hand. 'Nobody survived that night...' he said almost in a whisper, '...apart from one man.'

With that he turned and left.

I had cause to return to the island many times over the following years and always sought out this mysterious sailor to satisfy my need to hear the rest of the story. But I never found him, and my enquiries led me to believe that nobody on that island had ever seen him apart from me. Were it not for the sword he left for me with the innkeeper upon departing, which I still have, I would not believe my own memory now.

The End.

The Family Way
MEL FAWCETT

As her pregnancy drew slowly to its full term, Daniel's wife was naturally more concerned with her unborn child than with his carnal desires. Daniel accepted that this was as it should be, but he still found it a difficult time. It wasn't that he was insensitive; if it had been anyone other than himself, he would have said they were being selfish and immature - but it wasn't anyone else. He craved attention. He wanted someone to think about him and only him, someone who would be concerned solely with giving him pleasure, no matter how briefly. Yes, it was his wife's preoccupation with their unborn child that drove Daniel to do what he did. At least, that was how he justified his intention.

He thought a long time about how to proceed. Discretion was of prime importance. He considered going to London for the day, but he was worried that it might draw attention to himself at the office. Alternatively, he had heard that there were agencies who would send a girl to a hotel - it was Arnold, his sister's husband had once told him that - but he didn't like the idea of involving a whole organization.

In the end he went to a telephone box at the railway station where he remembered seeing cards advertising sexual services. The first one he saw had 'Your pleasure is my command' written on it. He scribbled down the name and number and hurried away.

Apart from feeling guilty about what he was contemplating, Daniel was nervous about stepping outside his usual sphere of activity. He was after all a small-town accountant, more used to looking at figures in books than lusting after female ones. He carried the number secreted in his wallet for two weeks before using it. Even then he dialled the number more than once and put the phone down a number of times before finally waiting with a frantically beating heart for someone to answer.

'Hello?' a man's voice said.

'I...I'm sorry, I must have the wrong number. I wanted Angela.'

'No, you've got the right number. She's busy.'

Daniel hesitated. He didn't feel comfortable discussing such a thing with another man. Besides, it was the strangest thing - the man sounded familiar and that was extremely unnerving.

'I'll phone some other time.'

'No, wait.' There was a pause. 'It's Dan, isn't it?'

'What!'

Daniel was alarmed, confused and embarrassed. He was ready to deny anything and everything.

'It's Arnold, Dan.'

'Arnold?' It really was him. Why? How? 'What...what on earth are you doing there?'

'It's a long story. Why not come over to the house for a drink later and I'll tell you all about it.'

'Oh I...'

'Don't worry, I won't tell Jean you've been phoning the local whores.' It was typical of him to relish Daniel's discomfort. Daniel had never liked his brother-in-law.

Arnold was from London originally and he had always struck Daniel as a shady character. He suspected Arnold of having some hold over his sister. Why else would she have married him? Sylvia had a forceful personality and wasn't someone to be pushed around. She dominated most people. Daniel had been truly shocked when she had married such a shady character as Arnold.

To Daniel's knowledge, Arnold had never held down a job for more than a few weeks and Daniel had always despaired of his sister being looked after. They were always hard up and never went on holiday - except this year. This year they had been to the Algarve, which presumably meant they had money for a change. Now Daniel was beginning to understand. He wasn't exactly surprised that Arnold had become a pimp.

He arrived punctually at seven-thirty as arranged. Sylvia let him in. She was wearing a tight black   dress and smiled at him so knowingly that he had to avert his eyes. They had obviously been discussing him, presumably laughing at him. He would have to say he had been phoning for a friend. Or better still, a client - so he wouldn't have to divulge a name.

'D'you want a drink, darling?'

'Oh...yes, sure, ' he said, 'I'll have a scotch,' taken aback by so many confusing messages. He'd never been offered a drink at Sylvia's before. Tea or coffee, yes, but nothing more. They had always been too mean or too broke to offer alcohol. And what was this 'darling'? She called him Danny, she always had. This had to be her slimy husband's influence.

'Where is he?'

'Arnold? He's upstairs. We thought it would be better if I spoke to you first.'

'Oh, so he's not working tonight?' he said as sarcastically as he could.

She ignored his question.

'Arnie and I have been wondering whether to tell you for some time,' she said.

She was drinking gin-and-tonic. He noticed she dipped the tip of her tongue into the drink before she had a sip. When had she started doing that?

'It started when Arnie lost his job last year. D'you remember? He came to see you.'

Daniel blushed. Arnold had come to see him for a loan and he had pretended to be going through a lean time himself.

'Anyway, we sat down and discussed things. We discussed everything. We were at it for days.'

That was what Arnold was good at, discussing things. As for actually doing anything, that was a different matter.

'Okay, so Arnold became a pimp, is that what you're trying to tell me?' Daniel said.

'Sort of...'

Sort of? The bastard couldn't even be a pimp in a straightforward way. He was probably getting someone else to do the pimping for him. Daniel recalled getting him a job as a night-watchman when he first arrived in town only to find that Arnold sold his shifts to other employees and so made money without doing anything.

'What d'you mean, sort of?'

'I mean, yes, he became a pimp. But you don't just become a pimp, do you? To be a pimp, you need a woman...'

'So?' he said impatiently. Then he stopped cold. All the confusing messages suddenly fell into place.

Sylvia smiled and winked and licked her lips with the tip of her tongue. He was reminded of a circus elephant he had once seen dancing in a field. It was both grotesque and sad.

'Oh no. No, not that.'

'Loosen up, darling.'

He must have been blind. His smarmy brother-in-law would do anything to avoid going to work and his sister would have no choice but to support him. It was all so obvious now.

'Why are you telling me this? I don't want to know.'

'Don't be silly, it's no big deal. The money's good, and it's providing a service.'

'A service!'

He almost said it's disgusting, but then he remembered that he had been phoning for that very same service.

'Who's idea was it?'

'What difference does that make?'

'It makes a difference to me.'

Then the door opened and Arnold came in. He exchanged glances with Sylvia, who nodded at him.

'Hello, Dan. You've got a drink, then?'

He was smiling, but Daniel could tell he was a little unsure of himself. And so he should have been.

'So, can we now expect business to increase, Dan, what with you recommending us to your rich clients?'

'I beg your pardon? We're talking about Sylvia, ' Daniel said.

'I know, she's my wife.'

'And my sister.'

'Don't come the heavy brother, darling,' she said. 'It's only a job. Which reminds me,' she said to Arnold, 'I've got to go.'

'Yes, all right.'

'You mean, you....you go out and do it?'

'Of course. You don't think I'd have a stream of men coming to the house, do you? '

'She goes to hotels, Dan; I've always insisted on that. Never in private homes or cars. If they can afford to screw my wife, they can afford a hotel, that's what I say.'

Daniel was having difficulty believing what he was hearing.

'You two boys enjoy yourselves and I'll see you later,' Sylvia said from the door.

'That's some woman!' Arnold said when she'd gone. 'By the way, I might have to dash up to the office if the phone rings. We had to have another line installed specially for that. It's not cheap running your own business.'

Daniel didn't know what to say.

'I'll tell you something, Dan, in many ways it's more difficult for me than it is for Sylvia.'

'What?' Daniel said, with ever-rising contempt.

'Well, think about it. She's out there doing it, getting laid and maybe even enjoying herself, while I'm stuck here worrying about her. It can be very stressful, you know. Not that we take chances. I wouldn't do that.'

'I don't know what to say,' Daniel said, embarrassed and appalled.

'Most people say, how much?' Arnold said with a laugh.

'How dare you!'

'What? What's the matter?'

'How dare you say such a thing to me!'

What're you getting so uptight about? Let's not forget that when you phoned earlier you wanted a whore yourself.'

'Maybe I did, but I didn't know Sylvia was one.'

'Did you care? We need money as much as anyone. Where were you when we needed it most?'

'What're you saying? It's my fault Sylvia's a...'

'Like you said, she's your sister.'

That was it. Beside himself with rage, Daniel jumped out of his chair and strode over towards Arnold with the intention of punching him in the face. Daniel didn't consider himself a violent man, but on this occasion he couldn't control himself any longer. But he was so tense, he tripped on a rug and tumbled forward more than walked. Arnold, sensing what his brother-in-law had in mind, was in the process of standing up when Daniel crashed into him. They both collapsed back into Arnold's chair.

'Jesus Christ!' Arnold cried as Daniel struggled to extricate himself. 'You've broken my back.'

Daniel ignored him. He was too embarrassed by his own clumsiness to continue with his violent intent, but he had no intention of doing anything to help him. While Arnold writhed in agony, Daniel left the room and then the house and slammed the door behind himself.

He didn't want to go home - he knew he wouldn't be able to conceal his agitation from Jean. But it was getting late and she would be worried and he had nowhere else to go.

'Something wrong?' Jean asked as he kissed her.

'I....I've just had a fight with Arnold. He made me so sick, I had to hit the slimy bastard.'

'What did he do?' she said, with mock-alarm.

'I...It doesn't matter.'

Jean frowned.

'You found out about Sylvia, didn't you?'

'You know?'

'Of course, I know.'

'But how do..? Doesn't it bother you?'

She shrugged.

'I think she's a fool to do it, but it doesn't actually bother me, no.'

'It doesn't bother you what that slime-bag of a husband is making her do?'

'Is that why you hit him? Poor Arnold.'

'What're you talking about?'

'No one's ever made Sylvia do anything, you know that. She's always done exactly what she wants to do.'

'What? He forced her into it! Didn't he? What are you saying?'

'I'm saying you probably shouldn't have hit Arnold. How did you find out, anyway?'

'Oh God, don't ask,' Daniel said, burying his head in his hands.

The end.

First Flame is the powerful debut short story collection by Bruce Harris. In this collection several well-rounded, memorable characters live out their lives in well-told stories that entertain and delight in situations masterfully observed and created.

All the 25 stories featured in *First Flame* have won prizes, commendations or listings in U.K. fiction competitions. They feature the variety of people, circumstances and settings which might be expected from a varied career. There are stories with multiple voices, male and female voices, humour, narrative and different generations.

First Flame has something for everyone, and can provide a useful guide to the kind of material which is likely to be successful in modern writing competitions.

Available at
www.amazon.com / www.amazon.co.uk
www.barnesandnoble.com / www.spmpublications.com

Damned on the Kitchen Floor
SHIKO

Noise echoes from the dripping kitchen tap. She hears Gianni swear at it from a distant place. She would be impervious to it, but for its sheer volume and she wonders how no one went mad. She feels nothing the kind of numbness when one has done something of terrible consequence that cannot be taken back.

Cindy's body lies before her, lifeless on the beautiful tiles like a misshapen doll. The body slouches sideways, its head jotting out at a terrible angle. Cindy's clothes are staining slowly with a viscous liquid. She thinks the liquid strange, with all its redness and slow movement. But for this and the body's strange contortion, she notices nothing. She has gone into a trance.

Jerking upwards, someone pulls hard at her armpits. It hurts, burns like scraping skin. She is hoisted against one of the curved kitchen walls. She too is like a doll. Stupidly her legs jot out before her so that the ankles face opposite directions.

Her legs are covered in the glutinous liquid and she reaches to touch. Though strange and alien, there is familiarity to it. Yes, that's it. It is like the test she does mid- month when searching for the signs of ovulation, when she sticks one finger inside her body, puts to finger thumb and separates them. If the liquid doesn't maintain viscosity for an inch then it means she won't get pregnant. Yes, that was it.

The liquid on her legs is changing consistency, becoming hard, coarse. It feels ugly, like the thing that had just passed. She does not like the ugliness. Outside the birds were singing their song. Were they replaying what had just happened? She wonders what on earth they could be so animated about and the very sound begins to irk her. She wants to kill the birds and is reminded of a moment of cruelty that has passed.

Acridity snaps her back into consciousness. It is the unmistakable smell of blood. Her mind drifts through the memories, of animals slaughtered in Africa before a feast. Long ago she had witnessed the event first hand. A large knife would be used, sharpened especially to slit the neck of the animal. The animal would bleat before its fate and blood would stream out onto the soft African grass.

That smell of blood was unforgettable. She blinks. Before her, Gianni is bent over the lifeless body. It is a strange sight.

'What are you doing?' she asks, innocently. Gianni retorts with a rapid scowl, turns and does not answer. She wonders why he looks at her thus.

'Fucking *mierda*! What have you done?' is all that comes out of his mouth in a loud and angry tone. It scares her and returns her to a motionless state. She dares not look to either side of her, just aware of those incessant birds outside. Wouldn't they shut up? She wants to kill them for sure and doesn't know why.

Gianni continues to stand over Cindy's motionless body, examining it. For what, she could not say. It was as if time had been suspended and they were both in some state of shock that warped the universe and made things temporarily go into limbo. Yes time stood still as she listened to the world go by. Outside cars were still arriving at the villa and she heard a splash in the pool. Time was only standing still for her, for Gianni.

Gianni was not moving from his position over Cindy and she was not moving from her position with her back against the cobbled wall. The pebbles behind her hurt her back reminded her of being in primary school. She had been shoved so hard against a schoolyard wall, so much so that it knocked the wind out of her lungs and made her fall into a collapsed heap. She did not fall into a collapsed heap now though. She was holding herself up with strong back muscles but her back hurt.

Tilting her head, she spotted the shiny bloodied knife on the floor. It was on those beautiful tiles, staining them, and she wondered how it had got there. The knife was a long blade butcher's knife and the end was very sharp. She could tell this from the thinness of its edge glistening in the Asian sunlight. The handle of the knife was wooden and bloodied.

Memories came fleeting back. That knife had been in her hands, her own hands, just moments ago. How had it got to that place on the floor in the space between Gianni and herself, and why was it so bloodied? Why was there an instrument of death lying there on the floor just feet away from her?

As if involuntarily she kicked out with one leg against the horrifying thing before her. Gianni suddenly turned at the action and looked more angered than ever. His face was going red and this was strange to her because his skin was so brown and tanned. She thought he was going to pick up the knife himself and kill her, stab her again and again in his fury. But he did not.

Gianni's face took on a different comportment. It became desperate, then sorrowful, then distraught. She wanted to go over to him and comfort him. He was still too close to the body and the knife was not far off. She did not trust his temper not to change instantaneously as it had been doing while time stopped.

Time was moving now and things took on movement. Cindy's dress was more and more bloodied by the second. It was as if it had been deliberately dyed the colour red. She wanted see what exactly was wrong with the girl but something inside told her that she, in some way, had been responsible for what lay before her.

The tiles were soaking up the blood now and she was thinking to herself that they would never be able to clean that colour out. She wanted to get up and move. She wanted to get up and start obsessively cleaning as she always did when she was nervous but even this seemed a feat too great for her.

'*Que has hecho?*' Gianni looks at her with a pleading look in his eyes. He knows that she cannot speak this language yet he addresses her in it anyway. She stares blankly back at him wondering what to say. She does not understand his meaning, the look in his eyes.

He goes back and leans over Cindy's now unmoving body. There is not a twitch or a quiver. She thinks that he and Cindy have a very strange relationship and wonders how it began. Perhaps it was in one of those seedy nightclubs in town where foreigners meet locals. Perhaps he was introduced to her.

Outside those infernal birds were still going and in a sudden fit of rage she jumps up from her seated position by the pebbles to grab the knife. Gianni gets to it first and the have a brief but feisty battle over it. Gianni, being stronger and larger than she, wins. He hits her across the face so hard with the wooden butt of the knife that she goes reeling across into the kitchen counter. She can feel a slight popping sound as her head hits the corner of the stone.

She wakes in a pool of blood. Her hair is in it and drying quickly, making some of it sticks out as if imbued with hair glue. One hand is on a gash in her head. She thinks of her own blood mixing with that of Cindy and in a selfish thought of self-preservation she wonders about her and Gianni's activities. She wonders about AIDS. She had seen too much of it when she was in Africa and it had scared her to death.

She lifts herself from the floor, sitting up. It's as far as she can get. Something is stopping her. Perhaps it is just lack of will power. Then she remembers the knife, that deadly knife. She remembers fighting with Gianni over it. She remembers his strong arm coming at her and her inability to move. Why did she not move? Why was she so powerless? Why was there so much blood?

Then the horrid image of Cindy's slumped over body comes back to her like a bad dream. She remembers now how Cindy's head had jotted out, how her dress had slowly turned red. She thinks of the exact moment that Cindy's body had stopped twitching and moving. Most of all then, she remembers the expression in Gianni's face. She thinks with an excruciating pain in her head of the question Gianni had asked her in his own language, in a language she did not understand. She holds her gashed head with one hand while a terrible horror takes over her. She looks around her.

Gianni is nowhere in sight.

The end.

"There is much to appreciate in Nduka's joyous language, his percussive rhythms; his sense of movement runs like a river..."

-Library Journal

"In *Nine East,* Nduka locates the grace of our graphic, bodied days, in verse somehow both free and arresting – volleyed between playful compound neologisms and stark, unaffected prose these lines capture the poet's life in all its quotidian wonder, the word recalling always our dual anatomies, formed of cell and sentence. The edges blur as we enter the pace of these pages, knowing ourselves here, asking ourselves (as Nduka asks himself, and us) why we are *waiting for a bus as the poem's face is lifting off, almost slipping out of the page, making room for the unintended.* They are poems for now, and for here."

- Lynne DeSilva-Johnson,
Managing Editor *Exit Strata*

Available at
www.amazon.com / www.amazon.co.uk
www.barnesandnoble.com / www.spmpublications.com

The Berries
PATRICIA MURRAY

Looking back to that time it seemed that the world was bathed in a golden light.

Nellie could remember many things about the end of that summer, not least the colours and the dwindling heat and the music. It had been one of those mid-70s hot spells, unexpected, unBritish. Now as the year progressed to its conclusion the early hints of autumn tinkered with trees and lured the tractors across the top fields of Grahams' farm. The closing down of seasons.

Dawdling through the small town streets of an evening, dodging the unruly gangs of infant hooligans standing round the chip shop doorway, dirty faces, waiting for trouble to brew from nowhere and create a diversion to their boredom, Nellie and Liz would swap judgements about their day at school: missing a place on the netball team; which boys fancied them; how Mr Brand, had managed to make hardnut Carla Kelman cry. So many things to remember. Abba stood victorious astride the charts, glittering and pastel, and clattering across neighbours' galvanized dustbin lids in time to *Dancing Queen* was the order of the day.

Sometimes they would come across other wanderers, soporific, slightly sweating from the exertion of running, most probably across consecutive gardens in the name of chap-door-run, getting on each other's nerves, like Billy Devaney and his sidekick Alan Forest. All from the same year in school, all desperate to be older or wiser or cooler. Desperate to be something.

One evening, meeting at the bottom of the road opposite Tom's corner shop, the four classmates leaned against the wall separating the old school house and the public library, not sure where to put themselves. 'Hey! I know!' said Billy, suddenly alerted to the possibilities this splendid autumn evening might promise and wishing to make some sort of impression on his peers. 'Let's walk up to the Den and see if we can find some brambles for eating.'

'Brambles?' Alan looked up, mouth shaping into a puzzled downward U. 'Are they the black ones that grow on the spiky bushes?'

'Yeah, black – sometimes red. Kind of bobbly-looking. You know, a bit like smaller rasps.' Nellie was the expert. Her dad was a gardener and there was nothing her jam-making gran didn't know about berries.

'Are they tasty, though?' asked Alan, who feared a wasted and uncomfortable trip all the way to the end of the town and into the wooded paths known locally as the Den so-called because of the gloom created there by the tall trees and high banks on each side of the path. Alan had been banned from going to the Den by his dad.

'They're the best. Really juicy and sweet, and my mouth's parched.' Billy was determined not to let this opportunity for entertainment slip by. It was only five o' clock. There were still four hours left of proper light and, even though they'd have to be in before then, there was plenty of time for something.

The foursome set off up the road, chattering sometimes, the girls listening with muted interest to the boys' odd conversations about nothing much: a new comic they'd ordered from Tom's, favourite football players, swear words they'd heard one of their dads shout at their Mum. Liz and Nellie walked side-by-side all the way whilst the boys changed their positions often, sometimes one at the front and the other trailing behind kicking a stone or picking up an interesting looking stick, or both at the back of the group, or one walking alongside the girls, listening in on what they were saying about who was cleverest in their class, which pupil Mr Brand liked best, what would be Number 1 on Sunday when the Top 40 was announced, and when the announcement came would they be quick enough to get the song taped, in entirety, on their cassette players?

After a while, Billy stopped short and pointed to either side of the path. 'See what I told you? There's flippin' loads of them!' And sure enough the children could see quite clearly that the bushes in front of them were crammed full of little shiny berry beads, mostly at the tops of the bushes, but still within reach.

It being still and warm all four had on shorts and t-shirts. Billy's had several types of stain on his and a selection of colours and shapes indicating this was not the first day the cotton shirt had been worn. This attire allowed maximum opportunity for naked flesh on arms and legs to be ripped mercilessly by the small but nasty thorns covering the branches and thicker stems of the plants.

'What shall we do with the ones we pick?' asked Lizzie.

'We'll eat them of course!' Billy tried to sound authoritative. He knew these girls; they were smart and he wasn't about to look like an idiot in front of them. They were in the same class as he was and had been for the past three years. He'd been aware somehow, without really knowing much about it, that they were becoming non-childlike, developing their conversation and their interests, filling out a bit physically so that the tiniest sign of a softer, slightly plumper figure could be seen emerging from beneath the thin cotton of their clothes. He knew that Mr Brand liked them because they were swatty, clever; they stuck in and were in the top group, the red group, and he was only in the green group – not even the blue, mind, but the group second to last. He wanted to show them that he too knew some things, that he knew about the berries first, that he had the idea to even come here, that the best thing to do with the berries was to blinking well eat them, of course! What a stupid question!

'We can't eat all of them,' said Liz sharply. 'For a start, I'm not even that hungry, and it'll take ages to pick them because you have to be so careful with the branches.'

Just as Billy was beginning to be annoyed by her irritatingly negative attitude and possibly quite accurate observation, the *whirr whurr* of furiously-pedalled bicycle wheels broke through the evening air. In a small puff of yellow path dust and a stifled screech of neglected brake blocks, the White twins, Charlie and Archie pulled up with a third, unknown child.

'What's going on then?' asked Archie, the eldest of the two as he stared at the four berry pickers, a bit hot and flustered now and with the distinctive purplish smears of berry juice dotted around the dry edges of their mouths and here and there on their once clean summer outfits.

"What's it look like?" ventured Billy not quite bravely enough. The White brothers were known to be a bit rough, especially Archie. He was in the first year at secondary and was already making a name for himself as someone not to be messed with, as the kind of boy who wasn't afraid of answering a teacher back and who would come out of a fight on the better side. Only last term he'd been belted for throwing snowballs at the school bus.

The third member of their party wasn't a local boy, but he looked similar somehow: straw-coloured, collar-length hair, freckled but pasty complexion and thin feminine-looking lips. A cousin perhaps.

'Looks like you're eating piss-covered berries.'

The four fruit lovers stared at the bike boys, wondering what was coming next.

'What do you mean?' Billy wasn't shocked by the language; it wasn't anything he hadn't heard before, but it was the idea of having eaten them – piss and all – if this was true.

Lizzie let out a feeble yelp and dropped the handful of freshly-picked fruit she had been holding so that they lay, partially coated in fine dust, a squashed heap at her feet. Nellie kept hold of hers but she could already feel their heat prickling behind the closed fingers of her hand. She wasn't afraid of these boys but they had introduced into this innocent summer evening an air of unpredictability which she found curious rather than frightening.

Archie settled himself back on his bike letting go of the handlebars and putting his hands on his hips, in charge.
'Don't you know, you lemons? Boys pee into bottles and then fling it over the bushes. So now you've been swallowing boys' urine!" He'd never seen the word before, but he knew the effect it would have and so took great pleasure in throwing it out at this bunch of babies from primary school.

Nameless boy, bored with this interchange between people he did not know, set his right foot on the top pedal of his bike ready to take off. 'Come on, Archie. Let's go.'
Archie pedalled towards Lizzie. He stopped just in front of her drawing his face so close to hers that she could feel the heat of his skin, and grinned. He wasn't bad looking. Then he stepped on the little heap of mangled brambles lying at her feet, squashing them flat and squeezing out a slurp of black juice.
'Berries are for babies,' he said. Then he pulled his bike around to face the direction of travel and rode off back down the path, taking his cronies with him.

'Do you think that's true?' asked Nellie, who held her empty but sticky hands away from her sides in case she covered her clothes in stains and boys' pee.

'Nah. They're just winding us up. I mean, you'd be able to smell it, wouldn't you?' offered Alan hopefully. He was way out of his depth here. He didn't care if it was true or not. He just didn't want his dad to find out that he'd even been to this place.

They all had a faint knowledge of the smell in question, and if they had not been children, perhaps they would have described it as slightly sweet, a little sharp and unpleasant, but certainly not the worst smell in the world.

Billy said nothing. He was standing in the middle of the path looking towards the space left by the bikes. Just a haze of golden dust swept up from the dirt path hung in the air where they had passed. Alan and Nellie stood quietly waiting for the next thing. 'I'm going home,' Lizzie stated. 'Before it's dark.'

So they abandoned their mission and started to trek towards their homes. The return journey wouldn't take as long . Nobody talked and Lizzie kept her hand closed tight around the berries, their heat prickling at her skin all the way back.

The end

The Lady Who Feeds the Squirrels
BELINDA RIMMER

Autumn is my favourite time of year. I spend my lunch breaks
walking in the park, admiring the leaves on the turn. That's why
I was in the park on Monday, on the day the woman went
missing. It's Wednesday and I'm back to watch the firemen
dredge the lake. So far, no body. The park stinks now the silt has
been disturbed. I head for the boathouse where the air's clearer.

When the police come to interview me later I'll tell them
everything I know. But it's not much.

*

On my way home from the office I buy some caramel slices and
fresh milk for the tea.

I've hardly boiled the kettle when there's a knock on the
door.

'Come in,' I say to PC Bradshaw in what I hope is a friendly
manner, 'I was just making tea.'

PC Bradshaw tells me he only drinks coffee and is keen to
get straight down to business. 'The missing person is called, Mrs
Virginia Hancock,' he tells me. He show me a picture. 'Do you
recognise her?'

'As a matter of fact, I do. She often feeds the squirrels from
a bag of peanuts,' I say. 'They come right over and eat out of her
hand.'

PC Bradshaw writes it down. 'Was she feeding the
squirrels on Monday?'

'I can't remember, exactly,' I say. 'The problem is, I walk in
the park most days. They all seem the same to me. My memory,
you know, it gets muddled.'

PC Bradshaw closes his notebook and says, 'Thank you for
your help, Mr Chase. I'll give you my phone number just in
case.'

*

It's the feature story in Thursday's edition of our local paper. I start to read aloud, though there's only the cat to listen. But then I get upset and have to make myself a strong mug of tea. I expect it's because I'm acquainted with the missing person. I almost said dead missing person. But I don't know if she's dead. No one does. I clear my throat and finish reading to the cat: *Virginia Mary Hancock, a part-time school nurse, didn't return home on Monday after her visit to the park. The police are treating her disappearance as suspicious. Her husband, Bill Hancock, a Geography teacher at the local comprehensive, said it's completely out of character. Her two grown up children, who both live abroad, are travelling home to be with their father.*

*

On Friday, I go back to the park, confident something will jog my memory. After a few laps of the lake I remember that on Monday Virginia wasn't feeding the squirrels. She was walking towards the boathouse.

I ring PC Bradshaw on my mobile.

'Sorry, he's away from his desk,' someone tells me. 'Is it an emergency?'

'I'm not sure. Can you ask him to ring me when he gets back?'

While I'm waiting for his call, I head for the boathouse. It's boarded up and has been for many years. Rats nest there and it's covered in graffiti. But a majestic old building is worth preserving, if you ask me.

Surely the police will have searched it already.

I step over the discarded bottles of cider and pull at the rotting door which gives way just enough to let me through. It's the smell that hits me first. Rat's pee, I tell myself. As soon as my eyes adjust to the gloom, I make out a shape slumped against the wall – a sack?

The sack makes a noise. 'Who's there?' I say.

The woman's head tilts to one side and she groans through the tape covering her mouth. Her coat is torn and there's a bruise under her eye. Her shoes hang limply at the end of her ripped tights and her ankles are tied together with orange rope. I guess her arms are tied with the same orange rope, though they're behind her back and out of sight.

'I won't hurt you,' I say, moving towards her. 'You're safe.'

She kicks out with her legs tied up with orange rope.

'Stop it,' I say.

Suddenly, I look around at the filth, the debris, the tied up woman, and none of it makes any sense. It's like looking through a fog. Except, I'm inside and there is no fog. I look at my hands. But they're not my hands. They're too far away from my body. Too indistinct. Whose hands are they? Then those hands, which are not my hands, are around the woman's neck. The woman mumbles through her taped up mouth while the hands, which are not my hands, squeeze harder.

When all the fight has gone from her, I place my ear close to her mouth, listen for a breath.

Nothing.

Slowly, the room comes back into focus – how long have I been squatting on the floor with my ear against a dead woman's mouth? How come there's dirt on the knees of my trousers?

I take out my mobile and phone for an ambulance.

*

PC Bradshaw tells me if I hadn't found her she'd be dead.

'She is dead,' I say.

'No,' he says, 'not quite. They haven't given up hope yet. Her husband's by her side and her two sons.' He tells me they're reading her John Betjeman poems and playing Glen Campbell CDs.

My heart starts to race – not dead! The hands, which were not my hands, were around her neck. My ear was against her mouth. The breath had stopped.

But what if she remembers those hands and that ear and the face that goes with them? What then?

*

PC Bradshaw says they're sorry they failed to include the boathouse in their search. He says they'll be making a formal apology to the family. He says they're sorry I had to be the one to find her. He says there's counselling available should I need it. I tell him, No thanks, I'll work it out in my own way.

*

The woman, Virginia Mary Hancock, is dead. She died last night. There's a full scale hunt for the murderer. Apparently, he, they're certain it is a he, attacked Virginia in the boathouse on two occasions. They think it was someone local. Someone who works close by, perhaps. Someone who spends a lot of time in the park.

I hope they catch him soon because no one feels safe anymore.

When it's all blown over I might take some flowers down to the lake and leave them outside the boathouse. I might take along a bag of peanuts too, in memory of the squirrel lady.

*

PC Bradshaw's says they need to ask me some more questions. 'Sorry,' he says, 'but you have to come to the station right away.' There's no time to make phone calls or feed the cat.

I tell him, 'Don't worry about it. I'm happy to help. It's a shame I can't remember much. I think it's common, these memory lapses, when you've been under stress.'

*

I've been arrested for the murder of Virginia Mary Hancock.

'You've got the wrong person,' I say to a man in uniform – someone senior to PC Bradshaw, I think. I tell him, 'I'd never do anything like that.'

They assign me a lawyer. She says, 'What's your name?'

'That's a very good question,' I say, 'and one that I'm happy to answer. My name is Jeremy Chase. I work in insurance. I have a cat. I do meals on wheels on my day off. I'm not a murderer. I'm just not the type.'

She says, 'Mr Chase, this doesn't look good. You do know you could be sent to prison for an indefinite length of time, don't you?'

'But I haven't done anything wrong,' I say. 'Since when was it a crime to find a victim and phone for an ambulance?'

We talk some more. I'm convivial but it always comes back to the same old thing – I can't remember what happened. But whatever it was, I didn't kill Virginia Mary Hancock.

*

The psychiatrist's name is Mr Edwards. Edward Edwards. What sort of a name is that?

He says, 'A guard will be present throughout your treatment. Do you understand what I'm saying?'

I say, 'No, not really.'

He talks to me about a lack of criminal responsibility, an absence of intent. He says something about a deeply divided person, a Dissociative Disorder. He says I'm unable to stand trial. He asks me lots of questions about my childhood. But there's nothing to tell.

'You're distraught,' Edward Edwards says, 'take a minute to compose yourself.'

I wonder what he means. I wonder why my face is wet. I wonder who's tears are running into my mouth. I don't understand. I don't understand any of it.

The End.

In this collection of poems, the reader is gripped and grabbed irrevocably by Obemata's matrix, nuanced and scintillating evocations on identity, home and exile in a globalised world with all its contradictions and ramifications for the post-colonial subject and his existential roving.

- Chijioke Uwasomba
Teacher and scholar,
Obafemi Awolowo University, Ile-Ife

In *Triptych*, Obemata spins pretty words and weaves them mysteriously into beautiful poems pregnant with profound meaning.

- Ikhide R. Ikheloa
Poet & critic

Available at
www.amazon.com / www.amazon.co.uk
www.barnesandnoble.com / www.spmpublications.com

Counting
HELEN HOLMES

She marshals her army of pots, tubes and brushes, squeezes six drops of liquid skin onto her fingers and works it into her face and neck. She tints her eyelids, outlines her eyes, blackens her lashes. She slicks her lips and blots her mouth with a tissue. A swipe of rouge to each cheekbone, and her camouflage is complete.

*

Harriet's stomach flutters with irritation as her headlights sweep across her neighbour's Honda. This is the third time she's got home after a hard day at the Resource Centre to find it in her space. She's mentioned it to him, but he doesn't seem to get it. 'No biggie, hinnie,' he said. 'Use mine. It's just as handy.' Which is true, but hardly the point. If everybody behaved like that, there'd be anarchy. Anyway, she mistrusts the number 5, a queasy, asymmetrical number. Number 8 is stable, reassuring. There are six stone steps up to the door of her flat. It's Friday, so she starts on the left foot, balancing cat-like on the balls of her feet to avoid the joins. She opens her door and steps into silence. She flicks on the light, deadlocks the door, checks the handle, puts the chain on. Stepping out of her shoes, left, right, she slides into the leather mules lined up under the coat-rack, left, right. She shrugs off her coat and hangs it on its hanger, buttons two buttons. In the shower-room she washes her hands, once, twice. In the bedroom she takes off her navy suit, brushes it, drapes it in a plastic tube and hangs it in the wardrobe. She pulls on neatly-pressed trousers and a cable-knit sweater. The room smells fusty, so she opens the fanlight before pulling down the blind. In the kitchen she leans over to open the window to dispel the smell of last night's haddock. She washes her hands. She takes out the green chopping-board and a sharp knife from the drawer and slices and dices with precision: one aubergine, one red pepper, one onion, two courgettes and three tomatoes. She warms olive oil and shunts in the vegetables, stirs and covers the pan. She takes a bottle of white wine from the fridge, unscrews the cap, pours a careful glass, screws the cap on, returns the bottle to the fridge. Standing at the window, she sips minutely, tastes apple and citrus fruits. A train clatters over the viaduct; bleached faces peer out of glaring windows. She glances at her watch. Four minutes late. The supermarket car-park below is clogged with weekend shoppers. Badly-stacked trolleys reel into the fairways. She must get a blind for this window now the nights are drawing in.

*

The day of Harriet's first GCSE exam, early morning was leaking into the room when her father stumbled in. She was barely awake. He tore the curtains back and turned to face her, silhouetted against the window.

'Shift yourself,' he said, 'idle little cow.' He spoke in the low, guttural monotone she dreaded.

'What time is it?' she asked.

'Time you got breakfast. Time you made yourself useful. Time you looked after your Dad for a change. Time you took your nose out of all those fucking books.'

'I've got to keep up with the work, Dad.'

He swayed to her desk, neatly organised with piles of text-books, files and paper, a mug bristling with pens and pencils, her lap-top winking a blue eye. He swiped the books, files and paper onto the floor, up-ended the mug. The lap-top came last.

*

Number 5 has moved out. On Saturday morning, Harriet snatches glimpses of the new resident slogging from car to building in the watery sunlight, humping carrier-bags and boxes, lampshades, brightly-coloured towels and bedding, an extravagant bunch of parrot tulips. She looks young, plump, disorganised.

Harriet has just settled down with her mid-morning mug of coffee and a book when the doorbell rings. Irritated, she centres her mug on a coaster and goes to the door. Through the spy-hole, she registers wild black hair and a grubby white tee-shirt. She opens the door.

'Hi! I'm Liz. Just moving in to Number 5.'

'Hello. I'm Harriet Patterson.'

'Sorry to bother you, Harriet, but can I borrow some milk? I'll pop down the Co-op later, but if I don't get some caffeine down me neck soon I'll start screaming and smashing things.'

Harriet is conscious of her own coffee cooling on the table.

'You'd better come in.'

'You're an angel of mercy.'

Harriet follows her guest into the living-room.

'Jeez, aren't you tidy?' Liz flops onto the cream settee.

Harriet flinches. 'You can have that mug. I haven't touched it. I'll make another.'

'Thanks, Harriet. Is it Harriet or Hattie?'

'Harriet.'

'Okey-dokey.' Liz gulps a mouthful of coffee. 'Got any sugar?'

'No. Sorry. I don't take it.'

'Never mind. I can drink it without. You haven't got any biccies, have you? Stomach thinks me throat's been cut.'

'I'm sure you realise,' Harriet can hold back no longer, 'that parking spaces correspond to flat numbers. So yours is Number 5.'

Liz blinks.

'I only mention it,' Harriet says, 'because there's been some confusion in the past.'

'Where the fuck've you been?' Harriet's father growled, his eyes not shifting from the television screen.

'In the library,' Harriet said, 'doing my homework.'

'What's stopping you doing your homework at home?'

'It's just easier to concentrate.'

'Oh, I get it. I should be sitting in silence in my own home so you can concentrate, should I?'

'No, Dad. That's why I go to the library. Anyway, I need access to a computer.'

'That's right, twist the knife. Have you ever thought how I might feel, coming in to an empty house? Nah, course you haven't. It's all about you, isn't it, Harriet? Like mother, like fucking daughter.'

*

'Thanks for showing me the sights, Harriet.'

Liz is slurping coffee at the kitchen window. Harriet is spinning out her tea-making ritual. The longer Liz can be penned in the kitchen, the less likely she is to slop coffee on the polished table or scuff the settee with muddy heels.

'Bit of a one-horse town, I'm afraid,' Harriet says.

'You feel a right berk, though, don't you? "Scuse me, can you tell me where the post office is?" "Scuse me, where can I buy a screwdriver?" It's been great to have the guided tour.'

'That's all right,' Harriet says. 'I didn't have anything much planned.'

'This is such a fantastic view. I wish I could see right across the valley.'

'I need a blind for that window,' Harriet says, 'But it's such an awkward shape, I can't work out how to fit one.'

'Oh, don't cover it up! It's beautiful. It's your window on the world.'

'People can see in from the viaduct after dark.'

Liz gapes. 'Harriet,' she says, 'This is a kitchen. What's to see? An onion orgy? A mushroom massacre? Anyway, the viaduct's about a hundred bloody yards away, you daft mare!'

For a second, Harriet bridles. Then she starts to laugh.

*

Sometimes, if Harriet left the library late enough, her father had fallen asleep by the time she got home and she could creep upstairs. Or he'd got bored and gone to the pub. Tonight, the lights were off, but the television was flickering. She eased the front door open and stepped into the hall. She could hear some game-show. The living-room door was ajar. She inched it open. He was flat on his back on the settee. On the floor she saw an empty whisky bottle. Another stood on the coffee-table, an inch left in the bottom. The ash-tray had spewed its contents. Débris from a take-away littered the table. He hadn't bothered with a plate or cutlery. The room reeked of alcohol, tobacco-smoke, greasy food. She was used to that. Tonight there was an overlay of something else: a childhood smell, a car-journey smell. Sick.

'Dad? Wake up, Dad. Daddy?'

*

Harriet is wrenched from sleep by the persistent ringing of the doorbell.

'Help!' Liz is even more dishevelled than usual. 'I've got a drama workshop, and the sodding car won't start. Can you give me a lift?'

'But—'

'Be a sport, Harriet. I've got twelve students turning up. I can't keep them hanging about in the car park. It's like bloody Siberia out here.'

'I'll be ready in twenty minutes.'

'I need to be there in ten!'

'But I'm not even—'

'Just sling a coat on. Please, Harriet. No-one's going to see your jim-jams.'

When they arrive at the Centre, Liz tumbles out.

'Harriet, you're a star. I owe you one ... another one. By the way, you look great without all that crap on your face.' She slams the car door. 'See ya!'

*

In Harriet's final year at school, the music teacher sweet-talked her into signing up for the chorus of the Mikado.

'Honestly, sir, it's not my sort of thing.'

'Oh, go on, Harriet. You've got a lovely voice.'

'I've got too much work to do.'

'Learning a few songs'll be a piece of cake for a clever girl like you.'

'But—'

'I can just see you in a kimono.'

As she shuffled onto the stage, she knew she should have trusted her instincts. She was a marionette, wooden limbs convulsive. Rehearsals were torture. On the day of the dress-rehearsal, the wardrobe-mistress allocated costumes. Harriet's kimono was royal blue with feathery gold motifs. She eased it round her dung-brown uniform, careful not to snag the silky material on her chewed nails.

'Harriet, I need to try out a chorus-girl's make-up. Can I practise on you?'

Harriet watched her reflection as her face mutated into a chalky mask, eyes black-etched blue lagoons, lips a bloody cupid's bow. Inscrutable. Her hair was swept off her face, plaited tightly down her back.

'Is that our Harriet?' twinkled the music teacher. 'I knew she'd look gorgeous.'

Her blush was scalding, but invisible.

Behind blinding stage-lights, her camouflage was complete. A confident stranger glided round the stage.

*

In the chaos of Liz's living-room, the wreckage of a take-away clutters the table. Harriet is helpless with laughter as Liz regales her with a tale from work.

'So I say to him, "Look, Marcus, please don't take this the wrong way, but I think you should, you know, cover up a bit more." I mean, Christ, Hat, it's a mixed group! Some of the women don't know where to look. Some of the men, come to that.'

Harriet mops her eyes on her sleeve. 'What did he say?' She reaches round the jug of daffodils for the wine-bottle, refills their glasses.

'"Well, Liz," he says, all hoity-toity, mind, "I apologise if I've caused offence."'

Harriet is giggling again.

'"But what some people fail to grasp, my dear," he says, dead patronising, "is that the human body is a work of art."'

Harriet shrieks.

'What I didn't say, Hat, and I hope you'll marvel at me self-control, what I didn't say was "The day your sorry body becomes a work of art, sunshine, is the day I sling meself off the bleeding pier."'

*

The scent of civic wallflowers perfumes the sunny room. Harriet is standing in a circle with ten other people. Eleven is a good number. Eleven people are smiling. Nine are listening to Liz's instructions. Harriet must concentrate.

'... dramatic language. Choose a word you r-r-relish. We'll go round the circle. Shout out your word, then we'll r-r-roll it r-r-round our mouths. Hands on diaphragms. I'll go first. LUGUBRIOUS.'

'LUG-U-U-B-R-RIOUS.'

'ULULATE.'

'U-U-L-U-LATE.'

'METAMORPHOSIS.'

'META-M-O-O-O-R-PHOSIS.'

Kindness
DEBORAH BIRCH

It wasn't like me to interfere, especially as they could have turned their hawkish bullying my way. I'd not had experience of handling teenagers, to my regret. Yet, there was something about the way his old body sank into itself; a jack-in-the-box retreating. Cowards. I urged the driver to stop and shooed them off the bus like pigeons. One spat at me but they all obeyed my pied-piper in reverse. Sitting down, I noticed they had peppered his hair and coat in a purple sticky substance. Blueberries. No child of mine, had I been granted the right, would have done such a deed.

"That was kind of you", he smiled. Within the expected shakiness of his voice I detected the respectability of a true English gent.

"Do you live near here? I'll help you home". I had no desire to reach my destination quickly.

I would have left him at his door, once he had fumbled his key into the lock. It was a pleasant mid-terrace with a small yard overflowing with beautiful, unruly flowers, unlike our barren detached.

"Come in, dear, for a cup of tea".

He stuttered past a darkened front-room, encumbered with heavy mahogany furniture. We entered a homely middle room with crotchet throws spread over chair-backs. An ornate table-cloth exerted the superiority of an over-size doily on a sideboard. Well-worn scatter-rugs adorned the floor whilst dimpled copper ornaments surrounded the fireplace. He carried on into the kitchen and I smelt the familiar incense from the match used to light the hob for the kettle.

"Are these photographs of your daughter?" Two framed images of a striking girl flanked a proud carriage-clock on the mantelpiece.

"Daughter? No, we never had a daughter". He reappeared, loosely holding a tin crammed with Viscounts. I politely declined and gestured towards the photographs. "Oh, Emily, my wife".

He sat down, gingerly at first and then with a thump when the safety of his cushion could be sensed beneath. We waited for the water to boil. Wisps of white hair and moist, blue eyes succeeded in softening his corrugated facial features. It was difficult to pin an age on him, perhaps eighties? He was entranced by Emily's picture. This was a kind, loving man. My husband could learn so much.

"Is she..." I wasn't sure how to ask.

"She passed away ten years ago. For the second time."

Using the chair's generous arms he started to heave himself up as the kettle whistled.

"No, please, let me" I urged him back down and approached the kitchen.

Every cup was filthy. A layer of house-dust and bugs had gathered. I filled the bowl and washed each one. It mattered not if I stayed here all day. Here was warmth.

We soon sat cupping our drinks. I had to ask.

"You said she passed away...for a second time?"

He nodded. "Deranged for forty years. I first lost Emily when she was thirty-six". His fingertips gently stroked his cup. "Then she changed". The words provided facts but his tenderness remained. There were no photographs of an older Emily in sight.

"Did she have to be looked after somewhere else?"

"I looked after her here". Then, as if to explain, he added "We were married".

His fingers struggled to remove the foil from his biscuit so I helped.

"Are you married, dear?" He wanted me to be happy. I couldn't disappoint. I was married, yes, I smiled. What I did not say was that I had *tried* to smile on our wedding day, on honeymoon, on many public occasions. Our early photographs reveal the effort. At the beginning, his smile was genuine. We don't have many pictures after the first year. His prying aunts and cousins made their snide remarks. He was wealthy and I was greedy. I'd married for money and security. It was untrue. I had married him for children. Wasn't that what marriage was for? Peter thought we should have romance, cultural trips, indulgence. He's stopped all that hedonistic nonsense now but he still won't grant me my one desire. What a selfish, unkind husband, when this gentleman so loved his wife that he sacrificed forty years of his life to her needs.

*

Some stains are stubborn. I take their resistance personally, knowing they cling to the surface to mock my efforts as I scrub. I was determined to lift the edge off this one today for Alf. We'd exchanged names when I came back for the third day. I couldn't see how he was coping by himself. Why should he? Such a kind man. It was only a matter of a few hours after work for me. I'd brought him a decent leg of lamb for tea tonight. We could have it together.

"Is your husband out this evening?" he called into the kitchen as both my elbows now worked the stain.

"Yes, he'll be working late" I lied. He'd be opening a tin wondering about my whereabouts. Well, if he will accuse me of being unable to control my emotions just because of one pathetic mug, my disappearance is his punishment. We didn't even like the damned mug. It had missed him by a hair, apparently. I'd replied, sarcastically, that I'd have to try harder next time. It was a joke.

I'd pledged to help Alf get his place clean. It can't be good for him to have all these germs around. Anyway, I found cleaning therapeutic. Idle hands and all that...

*

I'd been coming for two weeks now but Alf wasn't himself today. He was quiet and fragile, asking me questions and then getting distracted during my answers. We hadn't known each other long and already I could see a decline. His breathing was poor. This house was so stuffy. When I finally managed to force open his back door, the kitchen gratefully swallowed a huge gulp of fresh air. I brushed leaves from the step into the back yard. I paused, thinking I'd heard a baby's cry, but it could have been an animal. The vague fantasy of happening upon a baby bundled in a basket in the yard made me smile and then, as I looked up, I locked eyes with her. A wiry, clenched nosey-parker, about my age, early forties, peered over the wall. I couldn't imagine she'd have children either. I didn't suppose she would have the sufficient hip-size with which I was cruelly blessed, although I could only see her head and shoulders. She wasn't smiling, so I dropped mine.

"He does have relatives. Nieces". Her tone chastised me. "They'll be here alright, when it happens. You might want to think about that". A magpie landed on the back-gate of Alf's yard, distracting us as it dropped a shiny foil lid on the ground. We looked back at each other. "Vermin", she declared and marched indoors, slamming her door.

*

That same magpie returned for days, tapping at Alf's window. Alf made quite a friend of him. One day, Alf finished him off with a shovel. "He was beyond hope", Alf explained. "Only fair to put him out of his misery".

*

Despite his ailing sight, Alf still noticed the bandage on my hand.

"Have you fallen?" he asked, through heavy breath. Something bothered his neck so he cocked his head to one side, causing a permanent look of concern.

"It's a sprain", I said truthfully. "Badminton" I lied. When would I have time for badminton? I was either at work or here at Alf's. The scant time I spent at home was when I had suffered my injury. We'd got into such a row. He accused me of having an affair! How self-centred to think I would need a reason as strong as that to abandon him. Was it not enough that his presence irritated me? He even had the gall to suggest I was trying to get pregnant. He can't deny being aware of my needs. You know, it had occurred to me. One evening as Alf sat resting in his chair, his head slumped towards his left shoulder, I imagined what he used to look like. There were no photographs of him. I wondered about his former vitality....and what might be left. How easy would it be? I was attractive. There were similarities between Emily and me. Would it still be possible? His trousers sunk around his crotch, as if there was little there. Could he even remember what was there? I caught myself and this silliness and carried on dusting.

Of course, last night's row at home had developed and he'd driven me to the edge again. He shouldn't have stood so close to the oven. He caused the rage that forced me to slam his head into the hot, hard metal, straining my wrist in the process.

"That's why we can't have children", he'd whimpered through a bloody nose. "I'm being kind to us, to them".

"No", I'd screamed back, "That's why a child is what I need".

*

Alf is dying. I know. I've seen it before when my grandmother lay in her hospital bed. My mother put wet swabs on her tongue as her throat made a clicking noise. Then she clamped shut and refused. A gentle suicide. He was lying on the couch when I arrived. I stroked the wisps of hair that licked his sweaty forehead.

"Tell me - your husband", he asked. So I did. His lack of desire for a child. My anger. His premonition of a violent mother. The failed marriage. I think Alf appreciated the truth.

"Could he", he began. I held his head up so he could sip some water. "Could he be right?" Of course. My temper scared the hell out of me too. But was it selfish to want a child?

Alf looked straight at me. "So kind". His cerulean eyes showed gratitude. "One more kind deed?" He felt for the cushion under his arm and offered it to me. "I need to go", he pleaded.

I couldn't do it. Not to Alf, not to anyone. I told him so.

"Not hard", he said, coughing. "Sometimes", he breathed heavily, "right thing to do. Put me out of my misery".

I didn't need to refuse any more. Gradually, his face closed down, the corrugated lines relaxed and Alf expired.

I sat and looked at what used to be Alf, a dear friend I had made and lost in two months. I held his limp, skimmed-milk hand whilst minutes and half-hours seeped by.

*

It was months later when the police came. The female officer referred to the incident as 'historic', but she wanted to know what I'd seen. Well, as I never ventured upstairs in Alf's house, I couldn't help them.

The remains were found in a shoe-box, lying under a pristine cot. The body was severely decayed but they could still tell that the baby had been hours old when he was smothered.

It's none of my business, I know. I read the local papers tentatively as more lurid speculation about events from the 1960s poured out. Someone had come forward. Emily had confided in her about the baby's deformity and Alf's misdeed. He'd called it a mercy killing. Emily was never the same again.

They called it a nursery, this room that had sat above my head as I had variously cleaned, chatted to Alf and then stroked his forehead as he died. They said it was a room of purity and hope, coated in cream linen, with baby clothes strewn over the bars of a perfectly made-up crib.

*

I can't talk about it at home. We don't talk about much these days. We seem to have naturally portioned the house into his areas and mine, without saying a word. It's the spare, non-functional rooms that we go to, separately. In an optimistically purchased four-bedroom house, there's plenty of choice, and enough distance between the two of us, to imagine a completely different reality.

The End.

SPM PUBLICATIONS FICTION SERIES

Have you completed a collection of short stories or a new novel?

Are you looking for a publisher for your book of short or long fiction?

Have you considered SPM Publications?

Approach in writing in the first instance and let's talk about your book. It may just be the next book in the SPM Publications Fiction Series.

Send all enquiries to:
publisher@spmpublications.com

Dream Work
JOANNA CAMPBELL

Jason promises I can see his house when his folks are out. Says he'll kiss me. Half a pound of free sherbet. That's the price. Says his house is white, full of soft chairs and a refrigerator full of vanilla ice cream.

My face flames up when he's in the shop. He winks. Makes me real rude to him. But he sees clear through that. Jason ain't no one's fool.

But wanting ain't getting. Don't do no good being greedy. Jason's Pa wears a tie and drives a car out of the valley. Goes through a black door with a gold mail box. He lends poor folk money and waits behind the black door for paying back. His men wait in shadows. Mary's uncle passed clean out late at night. The neighbours said his jaw hung clean off. Teeth rattling all over the porch. He still don't speak none.

I work at the candy store, Jason, I told him. That's who I am. Wanted this job so long. Pouring mint sherbet into the little brass scales. Lining up jars of cherry canes. Running fingers through lemon sherbet; acid, biting.

"Just get me the sherbet, Emma."
"You have to bring the money, Jason."
"The sherbet, is all."
"I ain't some candy queen, handing out lollies. Ain't losing my job for you."
"Some yellow, some red."

I wake to the sound of the creek. Ma fries pancakes and the hot butter gets me jumping out of bed. I scatter corn for the chickens wide across the yard, then take my bread and a couple windfalls in a tin pail.

All through school days, breathing in the chalk dust, I sat dreaming of the candy store. Started work this summer, the sun blinding every step. But I don't need eyes. Know it too well. Turn right out the gate, through the dew-weighted grass, climb through the pines, cool and earthy, out onto the road, past the ginger cows, sharp right to cut through Banyard's farm, onto the short pasture where the sky hangs massive, the mountain-range a crayon-line in the haze, across to the school road and then on the track up to main street.

Seeing my old friends still filing into class, I have this sick feeling. Like I get when one has a new dress or a damn kitten. I have to find that smile. Just wish they wouldn't stare, kinda content, and swing their dinner pails. Thought how I'd see jealous eyes squinting as I strode past.

I think how bad I wanted to work. Work's all we got and we gotta do our all to keep it, Pa says.

Mr Prewitt's Candy Store sits between the Milk Bar and the Mercantile. Mr Prewitt's all clipped moustache and wing-collar. I always thought he wore one of those eye-glass things, like a professor, but he don't. He has blue doll's eyes and his nails are long points that scrape up the sherbet powder sticking to the scales. Makes you feel your back is bristling with horse hair. He pokes under his nails with a tooth pick to flick the dust back into the jars.

It sure is a clean shop. Not like the Milk Bar. I once had a pineapple shake with a knickers-hair floating all coiled on top.
I wear a white apron, gloves and a net. On my first day, the valley girls in summer frocks gaped from the doorway. I was kinda expecting that. But I was laughing. I had a real job of work. That crowd was living off their daddies.

Daddy's in the city, Mommy's wrapped in mink, But the rich baby's diaper Makes the same ole stink.

That's Pa's song.

Built like a bull, is Pa. Big curly beard. Just needs the cloven hoofs. He'd stamp 'em on our bit of turf, steam flaring outa his nostrils. Land is all, says Pa. Land is who we are.

He does his books on Fridays, turning pages and counting. His teeth tug out the whisky cork. The smell of paper and scotch is Friday. He rubbed whisky on my gums when my baby teeth were coming. Sometimes he shakes his head, says times is lean. Drinks straight from the neck of the bottle. Only sound is beard-scratching.

Sometimes pickings are rich. Ma smiles and makes me warm milk with honey. Pa grips her waist and waltzes her round. Lean or good, the smell of whisky lets me know Pa is in charge of things just as sure as any fat daddies from the valley.

Once a month I bring Pa a quarter licorice and Ma gets sugared ginger. My treat is their breath, hot and sweet, when they kiss me good-night. Ma says no girl from the valley could hold a candle to me.

Pa says Old Man Prewitt is a true self-made gentleman, 'though we all know fine well we'd never say nothing other than Mister to his face. Why, we don't have the vaguest notion of his first name. I just know he ain't no professor. And he ain't no gentleman.
His wife has hair black as a leather-jacket beetle under the wood pile, with a dark lace snood draping around. Her nose casts a shadow over her mouth, lips all puckered like she's crunching acid drops. Under her cloak, I catch a glimpse of jewels, glinting amber like a well-sucked barley sugar.

They stand an ox-width apart in their pew at Sunday chapel, like they don't want to catch the other's cold. She clutches her Bible, all fierce like a slab of concrete about to fall on her feet. Ma smiles at her all careful.

Those valley girls have been by again, bonnets in their hands and ribbons trailin', sayin' only maids wear pinafores and only granmas wear hair-nets.

Now I'm right grateful for my job, but weighing out their Parma Violets is getting hard. I feel like a lump of raw dough when they snatch up their candy and skip out into the sunshine, lace foamin' under their skirts.

I try thinking about Pa. How he went to Mister Prewitt, asking him to take me on and what an honour it is. Keep thinking of him twirling his hat in his fingers, saying 'Sir' all the while. And Mister Prewitt looking me up and down, up and down.

And now Jason's not making it easier, is all. I want him almost as bad as I wanted this job. Yesterday Mister Prewitt caught me poking out my tongue and all to Jason. Gave me that look. It says I'm hanging to this job by a skinny rope. He sure is light on his feet in back, behind the curtains. I never can tell when he puts his eyes to the slit between them.

This candy store is still my dream. But it seems kinda smaller than it did when I was at school. And there's a damp patch the shape of a three-headed rooster on the wall by the cash register. Today I hammer toffee into slices and tip sweet cigarettes into a basket, two for a cent. At closing for dinner time, the curtains open. Mr Prewitt re-ties my apron bow. After he jerks the loops into place, his hands feel like raw chops, soft and oozing, clamping my bare arms.

He pads across the way to the barber, sucking at the air like gravy. I see him settled in the window seat and the barber with his long scissors pointing at the moustache.

I turn the sign to Closed, hurry to the jars, weigh the sherbet. Spill a few ounces into the display. I blow. No time for nothing else. I twirl the paper bag so hard it tears. Close my finger over it.
I run to Jason's, sweat sprouting on my back, hair unravellin'. Down all the ways into the valley. I'm panting like a jackal, burning hot.

Jason laughs in that way rich folk do to make us feel we're worth more. Don't know if I like him now. He looks meaner on his porch under the shadow of the stone arch.

He invites me in. I'll see the house and go without giving in. I have to take the sherbet back. I want to see the refrigerator and lick ice cream in a soft chair, is all.

My apron looks grey in this glowing white house. Even Jason looks white, but kinda pasty. It's his eyes I'm scared of. There's greed in them.

His room's the size of our whole house and on the coverlet of his bed sits the biggest tin of chocolates. We sell that de-luxe brand in the store, but not this size.

"Can I see?"
"It's no big deal. Look if you want."
"Can I have one?"
"If you want." His mouth is creased up at one corner, like I entertain him.
"Changed my mind. I just wanna see inside, Jason."
"Old Prew don't sell tins this big in his tin-pot store. My Momma gets these from the city."

"Your *Momma*?"

"I mean Ma."

He's real red. I feel better and prise the lid off, wantin' the treacly perfume. Like when I started at the store. The smell throws me against him, powerful as the rankest cheese. Jason tips back his head and laughs 'til he nearly pukes, I swear.

A tin burstin' with socks awaitin' wash day. Guess his *Momma* can't stand the stink. Shuts them all away to fester. He grips me around the waist, whips me round to face him. He's staring at me like a butcher. Big pale eyes, ready for a feast. Just which of us folks ain't damn greedy? I can only think of Ma and Pa.

I slam the lid into Jason's laughing belly and run. I cut a straight groove out of that valley, lungs like sponge by the times I reach the store, just too late for Opening. I burst in, turn the sign right around. When I huff my ways to the counter, Mister Prewitt is stood there, looking at me in that way. And I still have the sherbet weeping into my palm, staining my skin like dirt.

Mister Prewitt says my job's almost beyond saving. I've stolen. And I look like a chewed-up toffee with my hair all wild and my clothes spotted with sweat and all.

Just what kinda girl am I?

He tells me to hold out my palm like I'm due a caning.

"I coulda had a beauty from the valley in here."

Damn couldn't. Hell would sell ice-popsicles first.

"This store is too fine for you."

Quick to forget, ain't he?

"Now, why would I keep a backwoods girl on, I wonder?" He's glidin' towards me, pleating a paper bag into a fan, nail-tips pinching the folds flat.

That bit of matting on the floor behind the counter, that weren't too fine for a girl like me.

"Looking very flushed, Emma. Need cooling down?" He wafts the fan across my face.

His hair looks like that shredded coconut, third shelf along. Desiccated.

"Better get behind the counter, girl."

He goes to the door, turns the key, turns the sign.

"Hurry."

His face is like a rough slab of nougat.

"That's it. You value this job, don't you?"

He tears my apron strings.

"This is what you farming girls understand, ain't it?"

His tongue yields like fruit gum. Blood as red as gob-stoppers, first jar, fifth shelf.

I leave him gagging on it. Spit blood on the floor. Stroll like a valley girl to the door, turning once to look back.

And that rooster looks kinda puffed up. Like he's crowing, asking with all his three freak heads what'll become of me. And what kinda girl, in God's name, will Ma and Pa see now?

The End.

There is the sense in this work of an involved and inclusive poetry, revelling in the humour, play and beauty of experience but also revealing moments of heart-rending loss and unfulfilment… a sense of poetry as story, constructing meaning and plot from the connected roles and all-significant affairs of its staged players. The poems go beyond their detailed representations of dislocation, personal and collective conflicts, to point a determined finger at the fragile moments and relationships which enact them. There is here not so much faith in the untainted breath as assurance in the possibility of recovery. In the cast of vulnerable human – and occasional animal – characters we soon recognise the dog across our street or someone we know. We catch glimpses of our own dramatic and unsettled lives.

Letter Home & Biafran Nights
Afam Akeh

Available at
www.amazon.com / www.amazon.co.uk
www.barnesandnoble.com / www.spmpublications.com

The Day a Heart Shifted
ALISON BOUHMID

That wasn't the hissing of steam. That was me, angry and bothered and hot. Even though the day was not yet. It would be though. It was going to be a scorcher, as my dad would have said. More from him later. One of those August dog days that occasionally steep the Parisian suburbs in mangy drowsiness. It was still early but I had been up for hours. I had never really been down. In frustration and ill-temper I was ironing. To get it out the way before the apartment became unbearable, in temperature.

I was ironing my husband's shirts. I was ironing his shirts for him. And wondering how this had come about. It certainly wasn't me that brought the ironing board to the household possessions when we pooled our single person resources. After all I was abroad. I had travelled to get far away from ironing boards. So if it wasn't me it must have been him, because the criss-cross legged monster was most definitely part of our domestic set-up. He must have done his own ironing before we lived together. Why was I the one smoothing out the creases? Did I decide to surprise him, when he got in from work one day, with a homely, freshly pressed, sweet-smelling bouquet of smooth shirts. When were desire and sex replaced by ironing? Was it a gradual process? A shirt at a time? Or a sudden, triumphant, heady wife love-offering? Were the two, ironing and passion, mutually incompatible in all households or did some couples manage to maintain sexual fantasies incorporating the ironing board?

Before ironing for my husband I had never ironed a thing in my life. My mother was an obsessive ironer to the point where she would not allow anyone anywhere near *her* ironing board. As a single woman, not ironing was a political act. I refused to wear the sort of clothes that needed to be ironed. The occasional show piece, I took to the dry cleaner's. I had other occupations, other pretensions. I was going to be different from my mother. I had been to university.

I don't doubt that my husband was a much better ironer than myself. What makes me think this? Well, he was always very nicely turned out when we met. And he was no longer living at home by then, so it couldn't have been his mother. He was such a meticulous man. The sort of man that empties all his drawers and has their contents washed and ironed before choosing what he puts in his suitcase. I was going to say that he was a patient man but that would not be right. Maybe he did lots of ironing and found it calming because I don't recall any rages in the beginning. Memory can be selective.

Whilst I was ironing my husband was in bed. On his own. Fast asleep. When it came to sleeping that man had a will of iron and I always gave up in the end. When I couldn't stand it anymore I would fall out of bed, a furious lump of a mother, to do what needed to be done, starting with bottles. But if I was going to be menial then I wanted to be excessive about it. To martyr myself and exalt in drudgery. To be able to throw the result of it literally back in his face. I wouldn't just take care of the babies, I would do the ironing too. Even though he... Instead of words, the thump and bang of the iron. The hiss. I was starting to work up a sweat.

I refused to let my anger be even slightly tempered by the knowledge that it really was better for him to sleep in. Oh, let me be frank. Better for me too. Once he was up I would have to watch myself. Watch him. As well as the babies, one of which was trying to stand up, using the lead and the board as leverage. Don't go being judgemental, now. I wouldn't have left those babies unattended so that they might seriously have hurt themselves with a hot iron. But flirting with danger, tempting fate, gave me a kick. It helped me stay awake and was proof of what I kept trying to tell him, forwards and backwards. That I couldn't look after the babies, and couldn't do the ironing as well, that I couldn't do everything I should do, that needed to be done, that if he wanted it to avoid an accident, he would have get out of bed and pull his weight, for I was finding it hard to cope and sometimes I ironed in the creases, rather than smoothing them out, only making things worse, much worse. Backwards and forwards, harder and harder went that iron. Crosser and crosser, 'til my heart it would burst. Anger was preferable to fear. My nightie was starting to stick to me.

I was never much good at pressing. I did not get the folds quite right and one end was always longer than the other, or wider. I folded shirts before putting them away in the Victorian pine drawers in our bedroom. There were other things that I would have liked to tuck away in those drawers. It made me feel inadequate, not getting the piles neat and tidy. But at the same time I harboured a profound mistrust of precision folding.

The phone rang. I pounced on it before it woke him up. Unexpectedness could make him vicious. The non-climbing baby started to mither. When I realised it was my father calling, I asked him to hold on a moment whilst I wedged the hand-set between my jaw and my shoulder. I picked up the baby in one arm and with a lurching action continued ironing. He was phoning from Le Havre where he and my mother had spent the night, waiting to catch the ferry back home. He was phoning from his mobile which was unusual for it was usually reserved for emergencies, because of the expense. They were sitting on a terrace having breakfast and the funniest thing had happened, whilst they were drinking their *café au lait* and eating continental croissants. A Frenchman had come up to them and started jabbering on at them. He kept pointing to my mother and saying Lady Di. My father thought this hilarious. Stupid fellow. He had tried to make the chap understand that she wasn't Lady Di and eventually he had given up and gone away. They were just going to have their third and last *café au lait*. They'd had a lovely time, nice seeing me and the kids, no mention of the son-in-law, but they did miss English food. My mother had a bit of an upset stomach. Both twins were squalling now, redly and damply, and I used them as an excuse to bid my father farewell.

When I put the phone done I switched on the radio. I had to turn it up quite loud in order to be able to hear. A terrible tragedy. Unbelievable. In Paris. The Ritz. Henri Paul. Oh la la. Oh la la ladi la. The princess is dead. Dead in the Alma tunnel, entombed in a BMW. Her heart displaced from left to right, tearing the pulmonary vein and the pericardium. Leave me alone, oh my God, were her last words.

I switched off the radio, unplugged the iron and picking up both of the howling children I sat down on the two-seater settee. They were heavy and one of them smelt ripe. So the Frenchman wasn't dim like my father had thought. He hadn't mistaken my seventy-year-old mother for the people's princess. He had been trying to break the news, to what he can only have concluded were particularly obtuse English people. Trying to do his civic duty. How had he known they were English? Apart from them talking to the waiter as if he were deaf and retarded? Their pinkness, their preciseness, their taking themselves for the centre of the world.

My mind drifted back to the ironing. How I had come to be the sort of woman who irons for a man whilst he takes refuge in his bed? Because I was my parents' daughter. I had fallen in love with my romantic ideal of a Gallic glamorous male and I had found his oddness normal because he was French. I had not understood. I had imagined that he would stop being what he was, when I finally grew-up and realised that something quite different was needed. He would magically transform himself into someone who, if I ironed shirts, would provide for, nurture and cherish myself and any eventual offspring that we might be blessed with. Someone a bit more like my father, even if I wasn't my mother. But although I had known what was expected of me, he had refused to play by the same rules. He had dug his heels in and proved to be everything except what I thought was decent, loving or normal. And it didn't matter how much ironing I did. Which explained my frustration.

He probably had never wanted me to iron his shirts for him in the first place, never mind marry him, but I had refused to listen. I had got swept off my feet by my own inventions. I thought back on the day of the wedding when he refused to come out the bathroom. Leave me alone, he had said. Or words to that effect. Somebody had literally broken the door down and dragged him out. It had all been taken as a fine joke. I had quietly tucked away that episode into the drawer until now.

I deserved to iron shirts. No, I'm being histrionic again, nobody deserves to iron shirts. Especially not for a sleeping man who is a stranger. Despite joint ownership of an apartment in an east Parisian suburb, a white Polo car and twins. I rubbed my cheek along the soft curls of our children before putting them down to tidy away the ironing board and its attendant paraphernalia. It was time for changing nappies. I would have to take them down five flights of stairs to the outside bin otherwise we would stew in the smell for the rest of the day. I resolved to listen more carefully next time and to stay calm and be clear. Leave me alone. Or next time I will report you? Out loud. I shushed our babies, suddenly nervous. I realised too late we had been making too much noise.

He came into the lounge, in his pyjamas, dully moving through his personal fog of fury and exhaustion. He located the source of his awakening and his eyes became focused. He scuttled towards us. The iron was still hot and I lifted it up in defence. He lunged and I smacked the iron down on his hand, branding him with a hiss. Our eyes met through a steam of hatred. There was a sickening singed smell. He will kill us, I thought, but I could not bear to press down any more, so I released him. He roared and grabbing his wrist with his unharmed hand rushed to put the burnt flesh under the tap. I could hear it sizzling. Shakily, I gathered the children to me. The running of the tap, the silent, gathering heat. A trickle of sweat down my breastbone. I wished I were dressed. He came back in and I stood up quickly, careful not to make eye contact. He had wrapped a tea towel around his wounded hand. Gently, I handed him his pile of pressed clothes, placing them in the crook of his arm. I told him that I would not be doing any more ironing. I'm sure that it was a look of relief he gave me before punching me in the face.

The End.

CLIVE BURSON-THOMAS

Morning milking

Mud mothers with slab shoulders they
barge across fields dense with dew
and green as the river that sings
in the copse. Slip-slop into the yard
on armoured hooves rich with earth,
manure and wet grass. They nod, twitch -
one rides bull on another
and they skate across the concrete.

Steam curls as they wrestle rough mouthfuls
of hay from the rack. Head into
flank I coax two teats until milk
chimes in the bucket. Sandpaper
tongues ruck up my neck and forearms,
fescue-sweet breath haloes my head.
On these mornings the world is warm
leather and my blood runs Jersey red.

F. PHILIP HOLLAND

Foxfire

There is that lope, that running trot,
as if the paw tracks burned them at their heels;
the old fable proved.

Two foxes, red-earthed, ruddy,
coming from the close, night-prisoned wood,
their flamed fur, scorched tip of tail, just visible.

The chilling dim backdrops an eerie theatre,
a rising-moonlight barely warms their courting place.
Flashed split-second of her backward glance,
and he, stilled, frozen, a forward hungered glare.

Smoke-white chests thump, and gingered edges
of soft bellies sear on their fleet-foot, sly-marauding need.

There is that burning power in her eyes,
she pauses, turns again, the slightest hesitation.
This feint argument no case against her scent,
which signals to the cudgel of his sanguine brain.

Faint wisps of condensation steam
from his lolled and most blood-thirsty tongue,
which, like a swift, red rag, quick-slips over slim jowls.
Those tearings at temporary rest, this hunger is more keen.

He must engage; the vixen tells him so,
screaming in her want of Spring,
a thin, high, eldritch yelp of heat.
His counterpoint; a tandem bark.
But as we peer, as thrilled and silent statues,
the embers of their conflagration disappear,

their ashes melt away; disdain to our awareness.
The masks that were, suddenly not even there.

And in the silent, blue-black sky
only a pallid moon remains,
like ice on fire.

CHRISTINE COLEMAN

An Arrangement of Bones in the British Museum

Skeleton of adult male in the remains of a basketwork coffin.
Lower Egypt. First Dynasty. c. 3,000 BC

Whose were the hands that cut the strips of willow
and whose were the fingers that wove them?
Did salty water sting their eyes as they sorted
the bundle of canes to be twisted and bound
into shape?
                Would that task have been part
of the ritual of the dead - a labour of respect
to be completed from the rising to the setting
of the sun, something to be shared between his
brothers and comrades, his sons and daughters
his woman, his whole tribe?
                Now you are here,
edge your way through the jostle of school boys.
Step close to this glass mausoleum and find
what has borrowed their fickle attention. Gaze
down at the exhibit. Read the label.
                Five thousand
years have gone by since they laid him to rest
in the earth, and here, on the remnants
of what they had woven, he is lying, curled up
with the top of a tibia lodged where
his nose used to be.
                The sections of his body
are presented half awry - here, some ribs
are still connected to their own vertebrae
but most are placed with all his other
separated bones.
                Even so, you can sense
that his knees were drawn up to his jaw

just as they were when those bones
were first mantled in flesh, cradled
in the fluid of his mother's
secret cave.

CAROLYN KING

Quarry

That day we scoured the woods in search of a murdered girl,
we were ill-prepared for our find.

Desolate autumn: cloying mud made heavy weather
of our climb, leaf-mould tracks dragging us down
as our faltering steps sunk into the slush.

Ten minutes, they'd said, from the road to the quarry;
but now the gradient snarled at our heels -
hostile, disparaging, slavering ill will.
Predictable rain threatened to call a halt to our hajj.

Under the tired leaf-canopy, we couldn't feel
the drizzle or hear the sound of weeping.
We dug in our heels at the prospect of giving ground.

Who'd have imagined her straying so far
from the beaten track?

And then we saw her - cold
at the foot of a crater: a hunted wood nymph
blending into the landscape of trees.

Yet not at all as I'd imagined her: gone the sketchbook,
the downcast eyes as she pencilled the likeness of yew and ash,
a Scandinavian student more accustomed to pine.

Grimmer - and even more bizarre - a worm-eaten teddy-bear
disintegrates at her feet; brought to the shrine
by grieving parents, to mark the place she died: remains
as grisly as any we might have envisaged.

The girl wide-eyed;   the tree stripped of its branches,
beautifully defaced,   still growing.

(A living-tree sculptor's memorial to a murdered Danish art student can be found in a deserted quarry on Brading Down, Isle of Wight.)

MARGARET EDDERSHAW

Hibiscus

In memory of my father

He always admired the hibiscus,
sheltered one on a window-sill,
where each flower's five spoon-shapes
in silky butterfly-white,
cupped by bright green sepals,
offered the open hand
of welcome.

From a deep red centre
radiated pale pink veins
and the sturdy pistil rose,
slim and erect as a flagpole,
topped by tiny red balls,
while pollen-dusted dots on stalks
spiralled the stamen,
like a diminutive bottle-brush.

He loved to watch the blooms
sigh
at the fading of their day,
gently twist
their papery petals,
now bruised by mauve,
curling edges
like moth-wings singed by flame;
then he'd chuckle
as these wrinkled ghosts
finally shook themselves
free of the plant.

When his head dints
the last pillow,
fingers spread across the sheet,
pale and innocent
as his favourite flower,
eyelids threaded
with delicate veins,
faded lips releasing
a sough of breath,
we wait for him to shudder
and fall softly to the earth.

ADRIAN K.S. SHAW

Holy Trinity

Bicarb, bleach, vinegar. Never a day went by.
You only have to mention them and I see her
      in her worn-out apron, kneeling on that cold floor,
      stockings laddered, dun scarf tied round her head,
      scrubbing the tiles as if there were no tomorrow.
I see the glimmer of polished brass and copper,
      the Stuart-crystal glasses, clear as a fortune,
the rows of gleaming pots and pans: her special pride.

And now, here, in this half-tended corner
      of remembered and forgotten humanity,
      her marble headstone shining in the rain,
as if reminding everyone: her family,
      her so-called friends, and all who criticised
such cleanliness, that it is next to piety in God's eyes.

MANDY PANNETT

A Marrying of Herbs

I'm making a soup, adding in carrots, coriander,
parsley and stock, sieving them all and musing on the word
dissolve which is an elusive, long-limbed word
languid as hush - but is also

a word for dispersal - a scatter of seeds
on too thin a soil, a small, pulled thread on a cardigan's hem
which begins its tedious unravelling

Better to see it as a dissolve: an overlap
of settings, a gradual transition from one image to the next
where the change in perspective is apparent
only when the film ends

There are measures of harshness here:
a dismal resolution as in a shrine dissolved, made
friable, disburdened of its monastery stone

Stone - too hard a sound:
dissolution should shine like a crystal of beryl
be sea-water blue and liquid
as aquamarine

O dissolvere, dissolvere -
are you a ripple from a gondolier's oar
or a subtle loosening of life
earth in Juliet's breath?

The Threat of Sweet Peas

Look closer. They're butterflies,
debutantes with untried wings
too scared to launch. They shiver
on thin stalks, neophytes

who don't trust air. They change
to lifeboat pods, curl up
in blueprints of themselves
- but in quintuplicate.

Not quite. Remember Darwin?
Mendel? Oddities possible.
Unexpected changes like:
these butterflies start flying.

Perhaps their eggs take root?
Green ribbons reach and cling
suppressing opposition.
- They mean to grab the light,

unfold their chrysalis-buds
as flowery Lepidoptera
(pretty, persistent, ubiquitous)
which colonise our land.

So what? Don't think of triffid
or piecemeal Armageddon
- just evolution plodding on,
taking what's left of us with it.

If homo sapiens must die out,
what better way to disappear
than skies of fluttering colour,
the scent of summer nights?

JULIE MELLOR

Meat

I had gone by too quickly to see the fall of his hand,
but in that split second of looking, I saw the cleaver
held high above a slab of meat: topside of beef
or a piece of pork ready to be cut into chops,

and in the space between my look and his hand,
were the butchers we used to have: Billy Hinchliffe,
his blood-stained apron and dripping hands, as though
he had been mauled in the abattoir round the back,

in the days when butchers did their own killing
and knew their beasts. Once, a bolt from his stun gun
flew through the neighbour's window and left a star
of shattered glass in its wake, too beautiful to repair.

There was Alf Marsden, whose shop had been a pub;
the smell of meat tainted with the stale smell of beer.
A bull of his once broke free and raged through the market
between the stalls selling ladies cardies and fruit and veg.

And there was Arnold Roberts, whose son delivered meat
in the boot of his taxi. He'd offer girls a lift to Barnsley
on a Friday night for fifty pence and a French kiss,
knock a pound off a leg of lamb, give his heart for free.

JOE HACKETT

Father's Knife: My Apples

Opened, to reveal your curved steel blade
suitable for pruning roses and words
from the page of my transgressions
as you clasp, unclasp, clasp again,
so old and well handled.

Closed, keeping your functions secret,
making me guess at your final shape
like guessing what's behind the bland
presenting face of the waning moon.

Open again, to slice out all juicy untruths.
Father, you'll eat them, familiar on your tongue.
You'll force-feed yourself my wriggling fibs
. one by one, speared on the cruel honed tip.
You'll slide them off with your lips,
never once touching metal,
entirely missing the bloody point.

Now, your bequested knife in my pocket,
there's no-one to tell me how to pick my apples.
No old man to tell me what I'm doing wrong.
How did that come about? Now I am the old man!

I push the picking pole with its cloth bag
up the tree, tug at the best Russets.
Dislodge one. It falls and I catch it.
Left-handed! And another. Unbruised .

NORMA POWERS

Sir Walter Raleigh – On his Portrait

I trusted the artist to do my portrait well:
velvet, lace, brocade, he paints with a kitten's tongue
and rapier's accuracy,
but, is my hand, truly so - small?

The lord knows, and all the court
that I have wielded sword and fought
many a bloody battle,
so why my effeminate hand?

He has my earring lustrous, my beard in trim,
pride in the posture, visage grim;
a man who cloaks a puddle
to save the slippers of a queen:
Flamboyance spread to stroke her vanity…
but not - Oh, not by that weak hand!

He gives no hint of risks I take
in questioning the status quo;
I hold life by a tassel's thread
and there this painter dare not go.
Even our bold virgin queen
will pause before an utterance
as closely as she spies her image in the
looking glass.

He will not dare the perilous waters of the mind,
to conquer foreign lands;
for this I lay no blame.

But oh - it is so poorly done:
That hesitant right hand.

Vengeance is Mine
VALERIE KNIGHT

Angus Vauxhall was the worst kind of bigot - a hard-drinking bigot. And, worse, a vengeful hard-drinking bigot, and a big fish in a small pond.

Squirreled away in the dark crevices of his mind lay a vast repository of quotations from the Good Book which he used with much self-important posturing to condemn everyone from his secretary (a 'Jezebel') to the deaf and dumb shoeshine boy in the bazaar (possessed by demons).

And since all exhortations to love and forgive had bypassed his own conscience, Angus felt justified, even happy, this morning as he busied himself plotting a nasty surprise for Hassan.

Hassan was everything that Angus was not - tall, handsome and irrepressibly good-humoured. And, being a devout Muslim, he prayed five times a day and eschewed all alcohol. At least, he claimed to eschew all alcohol.

And it was this that accounted for Angus's high spirits today because the 'sanctimonious heathen' had been drinking and Angus had the evidence. It was almost too much of a cliché - the level in the sherry decanter going down week by week - but the discovery had given Angus a self-satisfied buzz.

It was Hassan's hypocrisy which particularly appealed to Angus and which added a delightful frisson to his plotting on this beautifully sunny morning, when God was most definitely in His Heaven and all was right with the world. After all, hypocrisy was particularly reviled in the New Testament and thus Angus could be assured of a few extra 'Well done!'s when he eventually swept through the Pearly Gates in his company-issue Chevy. It escaped him entirely that there might be a certain hypocrisy in some of his own behaviours - his frequent visits to the local 'House of Ill Repute', for example, and the fact that most days he did his fair share of coveting. And, while he had never actually killed anyone, he nurtured many a murderous fantasy in his heart - and there was still plenty of time...

But none of this bothered Angus today as he drummed his stubby fingers on the mahogany desk and hummed 'Onward Christian Soldiers'. He gazed out at the dusty palm trees and surrendered to the pleasant task of pondering precisely how he would bring Hassan to his knees. He would have to be careful because Hassan was useful... Angus wouldn't want to lose him altogether, just bring him to heel and wipe the grin off his irritatingly cheerful face.

Angus was a small and vicious man, the product of a miserable childhood in pre-war Finchley where, having been much bullied, he metamorphosed from a stunted schoolboy into a pint-sized tyrant, and in 1948 joined Star Petroleum who were recruiting young clerks for their refinery in northern Iraq.

Now, eight years later, May 1956 to be precise, he had elbowed his way up to the dizzy heights of General Manager. His underlings gave him a wide berth and consoled themselves by clanning together and referring to him as 'Adolf. They did goose-stepping impersonations long before John Cleese came along to perfect the art, and blamed Angus's rage on 'SMS' (Small Man Syndrome).

On this particular morning Hassall, in his capacity as Angus's cook/houseboy, was going about his domestic duties with the light heart born of a clear conscience. First he chopped the mint for Sahib's lunchtime salad, then he picked a miniature lettuce from the patch he tended outside the kitchen door and mixed up a tangy French dressing. He changed the sheets, polished the brass-studded chest in the hall and threw together a pistachio pie. And of course he said his prayers - twice.

A couple of times a week, Hassan shared his morning duties with Jassim, the fourteen-year-old son of his sister Mehrshid. Although Hassan had never actually asked Angus's permission for this, he was satisfied that the deception was of no real consequence. After all, the boy was no trouble and had never displayed any of the deceitfulness of which Mehrshid frequently accused him. Hassan felt sorry for his young nephew and enjoyed observing the delight Jassim took in his fastidious dusting of the crystal decanters on Angus's imposing sideboard.

But today Hassan was alone and just as he was putting the ice-bucket ready on the bar, Angus, three miles away at his desk, sudddenly hit upon the perfect plan.

It was such a corker he could barely contain his excitement when he came home for lunch and was far too restless to take his customary siesta. And he scarcely slept that night either, so great was his glee, and he was up well before the alarm, like a child on Christmas Morning.

Tiptoeing through to the bar, he grasped the sherry, pulled out the heavy crystal stopper and carefully directed a stream of pungent early-morning urine into the decanter. Angus estimated the mixture to be about fifty-fifty and a perfect colour match.
Then, so as not to arouse Hassan's suspicions by overfilling the receptacle, he emptied a little of the noxious liquid into the sink and replaced the decanter beside the port. Then he resigned himself to having to wait patiently for something to happen.

As it turned out, he did not have to wait long...

Two days later Hassan fell ill with a fever. He languished on his narrow bed and Angus found himself in the uncomfortable position of having to minister to his servant with jugs of barley water. Hassan looked truly awful, sunken eyes, ashen skin, and once Angus had checked that, yes, the level in the decanter had indeed gone down again, he became truly anxious and called in Dr Natifi.

'A real puzzle,' said the doctor in his impeccable Oxford-English. 'If he's no better tomorrow we'll have to fly him down to Baghdad for tests.'

This possibility so alarmed Angus that he prayed extra hard and with particular obsequiousness that night and, sure enough, Hassan was better the next day, almost his old self in fact, and full of sincere apologies. And Angus, for his part, found his fury at the boy sharply intensified as soon as his anxiety had been dispelled.

'Thieving heathen bastard!' he muttered. 'Just you wait!'
And he topped up the decanter another inch.

When the level went down yet again the following week, Angus knew it was time for the final showdown. He would, of course, need a witness to Hassan's come-uppance, and he plumped for Miranda Scofield, an English widow who had stayed on after her husband's untimely death from an infected scorpion sting and who was the main focus of Angus's current coveting. Knowing the lady herself to be no slouch when it came to discipline (she had a maid and a gardener, both pleasingly cowed), she would surely be both impressed and amused by her suitor's deft handling of the 'Hassan situation'.

So Angus set about organising a little dinner-for-two and Hassan was busy for days preparing the four-course meal. Everything went like clockwork, the only truly anxious moment coming at the beginning of the evening when it seemed that Mrs Scofield was going to insist on sherry as an aperitif. Sweating with horror, Angus assured her that an ice-cold martini would be much more appropriate on such a warm evening and to his enormous relief she relented and even twiddled her olive-on-a-stick in a gratifyingly coquettish manner.

She also laughed at all his jokes and listened, spellbound, as he droned on about his heroic climb up the managerial ladder. She ate and drank heartily and became almost skittish, once even patting him on the arm and calling him 'a naughty boy'.

By the end of the third course and much stimulated by wine and excitement, Angus could wait no longer. His Big Moment had arrived.

'Hassan!' he bellowed, startling the boy who was carefully placing two liqueur glasses on the sideboard. 'I've got a bone to pick with you! - and I want to sort it out now while Mrs Scofield is here...'

'Sahib...?' Hassan whispered, turning from the sideboard and visibly shaking in his shoes. 'Was everything not to your liking?'
'Oh, everything was fine, absolutely bloody fine!' Angus hissed through clenched teeth. 'But what I want to know is this - what possessed you to think you could swig my sherry when my back was turned? Eh...? Eh...?'

He jabbed his forefinger in the air and then, glancing puckishly at Mrs Scofield, continued at full volume. 'D'you want to know what you've been drinking?'

Sitting up tall for maximum effect (he was, after all, only five-foot-three), Angus squared his little shoulders and continued: 'Don't even think of denying it, boy, you're the only other person who goes near the bar in this house and, as you well know, 1 only drink vino and spirits... and ... ' he spluttered, raising the

decibels yet again, 'I was clever, you see... I marked the side of the decanter... and the level's been going down week by week...'
And he snorted like an inebriated wart-hog.

'Oh Sahib! Sahib!' Hassan exclaimed, his face radiant with joyous relief, 'Oh my good Sahib, please do not concern yourself, See! - This is where your sherry has gone!'
And he proudly indicated the elaborately decorated dessert in its crystal bowl which he had carefully placed on the mat at the centre of the table. 'I have been pouring sherry on to the sponge every day for three weeks, as you once told me to and...'

But, before he could finish, Miranda Scofield had grasped the serving spoon and was plunging it into the rich, creamy confection. 'My absolute favourite!' she cried in delight. 'A real sherry trifle! Oh Angus, you are such a naughty boy!'

The Lure
VALERIE KNIGHT

The woman sitting on the little balcony raised her face to the early morning sun and closed her eyes. The golden warmth soothed her and she stretched her arms above her head, blissfully unaware of the steely eyes observing her every move.
She was new to the area - new and lonely and rather tired. But, then, as she constantly reminded herself, it was always like this in a new town. Things would improve. She would regain her strength, make friends, come to a plateau of comfortable familiarity with these strange streets and new faces.

'This too will pass,' she murmured as she breathed in the unusual scents and listened to the unfamiliar birdcalls. She was of indeterminate age, between 50 and 60, a little late for fresh starts she thought, but perhaps not too late.

Each day she walked on the beach, the foam bubbling between her toes, and she began to notice which tides brought in the seaweed and from which direction the breezes came. Then she would climb to the top of the cliff, up the long wooden staircase, and sit on the slatted bench looking out over the expanse of ocean while the sand dried on her feet. Her gaze would settle on the thin line of the horizon and she would allow herself to be hypnotised into a dreamy trance by the turquoise and indigo swell.

Until one day a voice from behind her broke through the stillness and startled her out of her reverie.

'Another beautiful day in Paradise!' the voice said, with a lilt that lightened her heart so that she turned round like a child expecting a glad surprise.

She found herself looking into the bronzed face of a man carrying a fishing rod and a bucket. He wore shorts and a brightly coloured shirt, and on his head a battered black cap. His lips were full and smiling and she liked his face even though she couldn't see his eyes which were screened behind wraparound dark glasses, the kind you buy at the cancer prevention shop.

'Been in ?' he asked, jerking his head in the direction of the sea, 'been swimming?'

'No!' she said with a shudder, 'too cold for me!'

He grunted and sat down beside her, the fishing-rod between his knees, his profile enigmatic. 'New around here ?'

She nodded.

'Thought so.'

'Caught anything?' she asked shyly from under her sunhat. 'Any fish in the bucket ?'

'No, I'm just on my way to my fishing-place - I saw you sitting here so I pulled up.'

She turned and noticed an old open-tray van parked a few yards away and was momentarily puzzled that she hadn't heard him arrive - trucks like that rattled.

'So why did you bring your bucket and rod?' she asked. 'Why get them out now if you're still on your way to your fishing place?'

'Force of habit I s'pose,' he replied, unperturbed. A small smile played on his lips and his gaze remained fixed on the horizon as he added, 'I live next door to you - did you know?'

'No!' she exclaimed. 'There's a nurse in the flat next to me...'

'I didn't mean the next door flat,' he interjected, shifting the bucket slightly with his foot, 'I live in the next block - Number Five - second floor. I can see your front door from my balcony, I see you coming and going, I recognized the pink hat just now as I was passing.'

And then, as suddenly as he had arrived, he stood up and made off towards the van. 'See you again,' he said. And then, as an afterthought: 'Come up for a drink this evening - about 6.30 - Flat Five.'

It wasn't a question, he knew she would come.

*****

Later, as he stood pouring cold lager, she glanced round the room, noticing how few possessions he had, how it looked as if he, too, had just moved in. And as if catching her unasked question, he handed her the glass and said, 'Been here three years - I like to keep things simple. More time to do things that way...'

She nodded, her attention momentarily distracted by a small brightly painted wooden object on the table in front of her. It reminded her of the sort of earring she might have bought at a craft fair and she reached forward to pick it up. 'What's this?' she asked, caressing it in her palm, enjoying the feel of it.

'That's a popper,' he said, 'I make my own. It's a lure for catching fish with - these are all lures...' And he handed her a small basket filled with what looked like broken Christmas tree baubles, or perhaps pieces of a child's toy from a bygone age.

Little spangled bits of metal, feathers, brightly painted beads, and miniature fish - golden with ruby eyes, or silver embedded with what looked like emeralds.

'They're pretty,' she said, enchanted; and he replied, 'The fish think so too.'

'Are some better than others?' she asked, toying with a tiny silver spoon which had been bent, Uri-Geller-style, into a fishy-shape.

'Not really,' he replied, draining his glass and going back to the fridge, 'I choose the right one for the day, that's all.'

'And is it always the right one?' she asked, her head on one side, teasing.

'Always,' he said, not teasing in the least, 'the right one calls to me every time...' He looked directly at her, 'Why not come with me tomorrow?'

'Oh, I don't know,' she hesitated, 'I don't think I'd be keen on fishing.'

'You don't have to be - I'll fish and you can swim.'
'But you know it's too cold for me to swim.'

'Not where I go - trust me...'

And so it was that next morning she found herself sitting on a little patch of sand on a sheltered bend in the river. The man was standing a few yards away, motionless, holding his fishing-rod, his eyes screened as usual, and the calm estuary water was indeed very warm. She eased a foot in, and then a leg, felt the smooth flat stones on the bottom, and then all of a sudden she was floating effortlessly, her face bathed in sunshine, her body lapped by the gentle motion of the water. And, afterwards, as they sat side by side on the sand, drinking tea from a thermos she had packed in her basket, he showed her what he used for bait.

'It's a secret,' he said with a chuckle, 'you mustn't tell a soul!' And she felt honoured to be thus trusted as he showed her the strange and sticky mixture at the bottom of an old ice-cream carton. 'Breadcrumbs and molasses!' he announced, 'they love it!' And he roared with laughter, throaty and savage, yet oddly endearing.

Without realizing quite how it had happened, the fishing-trips had become a daily ritual and six weeks had gone by and she felt uneasy, sensing she was not a willing participant but, rather, a part of this ritual, like a chalice or a vestment. Also with a small stab of shame she confessed to herself that she wanted the man and that he knew she wanted him but he wasn't going to be had on any terms but his own.

Lying in bed at night, sleepless with longing and aware of a sharp little pain in her heart, she chided herself for her folly, for being that most pathetic of creatures - a spinster in late middle age, bewitched by the attentions of a younger man. And she visualised his strong legs as he stood in the water, the muscles in his arms as he cast the line, the occasional sardonic smile, worst and indeed most tantalising of all, she would remember the pressure of his lips and the saltiness of his mouth for, yes, he had kissed her. He had kissed her more than once, and always when she least expected it, when she was least prepared. He would kiss her at the precise moment when she had decided once and for all to withdraw. Each time she resolved to free herself - to go to a different beach, to seek out new friends - he would kiss her, each time a little more urgently, as if promising, promising, promising... and she would find herself drowning in wave upon wave of desire. Then, as unexpectedly and suddenly as the kiss itself, would come the icy chill of rejection - just enough to break her spirit without breaking his hold.

And the sharp little pain in her heart became sharper still with each passing day so that sometimes she was forced to crouch under the shower until the hot water streaming over her trembling, lonely body soothed her so she could breathe again.

But one day it was suddenly too much to bear and she knew that the pain of hanging on to the illusion must surely be greater than the pain of relinquishing it for ever.

It was early evening and she rocked back and forth, back and forth, on the thin carpet. 'This too will pass, this too will pass...' she intoned. But her tears, salty as the sea, made a mockery of the words and so she gave up and hugged her knees as the sun went down over the Norfolk Island pines. When it was finally dark, she knew she must go to him and in firm tones express her new resolve. All the time the sharp little pain in her heart tightened until she could scarcely breathe.
Sobbing for air, she stumbled out of the front door on to the outside walkway and then down the flight of steps, clutching the cold metal rail. And when she reached the bottom, the pain made her cry out in odd little gasps as she half-ran, half-crawled across the scrubby grass towards the block where he lived, her mind already forming the words with which she would reclaim herself. The scene would be one of high drama for he would understand and thus would be ennobled, while she would walk away, her dignity intact.

But as she reached the grass verge, the cramping in her chest reached such a crescendo of agony that the imagined words took flight and she found herself sinking into an ocean of stars.

*****

People came running, two or three, then half a dozen, and then reassuring men in white uniforms tipped out of an ambulance and began to do complicated things in the dark with gadgets and blankets and low voices. Until one of them said, more anxiously now, 'We're losing her... we're losing her...' and everyone was too busy to look up to the second-floor window but if they had done so they would have seen a man smiling with a certain triumph as he scaled and gutted today's catch into the stainless steel sink.

*****

Much later, a young man in a crisp lab coat stood looking at the body of the woman laid out on the slab and felt strangely moved. She lay as if asleep on the beach after a refreshing dip - pearly white pelvis and breasts; golden limbs, midriff and face; hair tawny and unkempt. And he felt an almost reverential apprehension, as he pressed the knife into the cold flesh.

*****

Nobody remarked on the strange mixture of bread and molasses which was all the woman's stomach contained, but medical students do marvel at the phenomenon of her heart which now resides in a jar at the University of Western Australia. They puzzle over the spectacle of an organ embedded with dozens of small hooks - shiny shards of metal, sharp and jagged, which shred the delicate pink tissue, and make neat fissures, little bleeding slits - each one the gaping mouth of a dying fish.

The End

MANDY PANNETT

ALL THE INVISIBLES

Light is threaded through Mandy Pannett's poems, along with a tantalising sense of individuals captured momentarily in many different landscapes, among them, the artists, Durer, Seurat, Monet and Ravilious.

Her language is visual and athletic with metaphor, she's drawn to lost traditions and phrases and brings them into the present with a playful sense of inquiry.

This book moves through a range of emotional states - all of them bittersweet: melancholy, change, curiosity - but Pannett is spare with words and her lines feel charged as a result. Expect to be startled by the images she creates, intrigued and excited by her talent for description and the insights her poems offer you, like delicious, rare fruit.
- **Jackie Wills**

Available at
www.amazon.com / www.amazon.co.uk
www.barnesandnoble.com / www.spmpublications.com

Mr Carrington
ANNE OATLEY

The girls at school thought playing the violin was square, but I didn't care. They couldn't understand why I found practicing for hours more exciting than talking about which of the Monkees we fancied most, or whether we'd rather snog David McCallum out of *Man from U.N.C.L.E.* I sat through double history, still feeling the nudge of the instrument under my chin. I played in my dreams, too, but there it always went wrong. I'd be in front of an audience and realize I didn't know the piece, or I'd put my bow to the strings and tortured cat noises would come out. When I woke up, shaken, I had to replay Mr Carrington's beautiful actor's voice in my head, telling me what a sensitive player I was, how he'd never heard such expression in someone so young. I felt embarrassed when he praised me, as if the whole world was pointing at me, but lifted up and happy too. I got the same feelings when I heard his name, though it was usually Mum asking me if I'd had a good lesson and not waiting for the answer.

The first few times I went to Mr Carrington's house, I used to go pink and look at the floor when I had to speak to him. I relaxed a bit when he started giving me lifts home. He said he didn't like to think of me waiting at the bus stop after dark. He always talked to Mum on the doorstep, and I was glad she was seeing a bit of how wonderful he was. My brother was jealous, chanting, 'You're in love with Mr Carrington. He's your boyfriend.' But that was silly, because I was a baby then, only eight.

Mum told me I should be grateful Mr Carrington took such trouble over me, but her face lit up when he praised my playing. I heard her murmur the word 'gifted' to her friends. So she didn't mind when he took me to concerts in Birmingham, even though that meant being out on a school night. We saw

Menuhin himself once, but my favourite performer was Iona Brown, because she was young and English. The drive was almost better than the concert, talking all the way, me sitting in front with Mr Carrington, the way Mum did with Dad. When a square flat package arrived for my eleventh birthday, I ripped off the paper to run my fingers over the misty black-and-white profile on the sleeve. The card said 'To a future Iona.' I wore the record out on our radiogram, and Mum didn't have to nag me to write a thank-you letter.

Three years later, I was still trying to explain what the lessons meant to me. I remember talking to Mum and Dad over dinner about learning a Chopin nocturne, how I didn't know if it was any good, but I poured myself in and hoped what I felt about the music came out.

Mum said, 'Yes, Chopin is lovely. Elbows off the table, dear. Aren't you going to have some of that nice cauliflower?'

Dad said, 'Getting a bit intense, eh, Sausage?'

But I'd learned to laugh with Mr Carrington at 'the good citizens of Tewkesbury, who send their little darlings to me, because learning the violin is *naice*. Musical as lamp-posts, most of them.'

It must have been hard for him, when he'd been to the Royal College of Music, and played with the London Philharmonic, to end up giving private lessons in a small town. Once I asked him why, and he shrugged. 'Careers get derailed. And you can have enough of London, really.'

Then he started talking about relaxation exercises that would help me with my vibrato, and I gave up asking questions, because when he talked about playing all I could do was listen, glowing that someone who knew so much should bother with me.

So I knew a bit about his past. I could tell he wasn't old like Mum and Dad, but he wasn't really young either. And I knew his first name, from the letters on his hall table. Disappointingly, it was Graham, but you didn't call adults by their first name anyway. I learned something about him from the practice room, the only room in his house I saw. On the walls there were pictures in frames that had actually been painted, and the furniture looked different from home because it was antique. Apart from that, all I knew was that he had a long pale profile and dark hair that flopped over his forehead. I had to shut those out when I was playing and keep my eyes on the score, but the thought that he was watching kept me going, like a spell.

Now I was fourteen, and I'd travelled so far with Mr Carrington, from the first screeching exercises to Vivaldi, advanced stuff for my age. Other changes were happening, exciting ones. Mum took me to Gamages in Gloucester to buy my first bra, a strip of lace and elastic. There was a box of unmentionable cotton wool things in my cupboard. I was a woman now, like Brigitte Bardot gazing sleepily from a poster, or the dancers on Top of the Pops kicking their glossy legs. I pored over magazines, yearning for knee-high boots and silver lipstick. Some girls at school had parents who let them have parties with boys, and they had giggly conversations about how to kiss with your mouth open. And I'd worked out what I felt about Mr Carrington, and I wanted to do something about it.

Just my luck that he was well-known in Tewkesbury now, so he had loads more pupils and didn't have time to take me to concerts. He still gave me my lift home when he could, but that went horribly wrong one night. I'd blundered my way through the lesson, because the evening was warm, and I always got distracted when he took his tweed jacket off and taught in his shirtsleeves. I'd been thinking of him the night before, in bed I mean, and I worried he could tell. Once we were in the car, he turned the radio on instead of talking, and *Hey Jude* was playing. I'd loved the song the first time I heard it, a couple of days ago.

The intro was so simple, as if the singer was having a conversation, and then the chorus opened around you, like seeing the sea for the first time. I couldn't help joining in with the la-las. Mr Carrington's hand shot towards the knob. 'I can't believe someone like you can listen to that-dross,' he snapped, without taking his eyes from the road. For a moment, he could have been any adult telling me off.

He didn't say anything for the rest of the drive, and when my next lesson came round I worked desperately at my staccato to make it up to him. I was staring so hard at the score the staves were wobbling on the page, but I felt a warmth next to me, and I knew he had got up and was standing at my side. He moved his hands around my shoulders, correcting my position, and the gap between his fingertips and my skin fizzed. Out of the corner of my eye, I could see his cheek, the tiny pores like glove-leather. With a rush of hormones, I kissed him. Yes, I did. My lips splashed, half on his mouth and half on his chin. We froze together for a second. Then he pulled his head back and stared at me, his face rigid.

I grabbed the score, bundled my violin into its case, and ran out of the room in one movement. I was still blushing when the bus dropped me outside my front gate.

School had broken up for the summer, and I spent the next few days either in my room or walking our cocker spaniel until he was footsore. I shifted every detail of that last lesson around in my mind, like pieces in a kaleidoscope, trying to make them into something that wouldn't hurt. I half-convinced myself that he was holding back out of guilt, because of my age. Then I looked at the shelf of dolls I still kept above my bed, and wondered why I could have imagined he'd be interested in a silly little girl like me. Born too late. I tried to forget how much the straight line of his mouth had looked like disgust. To make things worse, I was going to miss the next lesson, because we were going out for a meal for Dad's birthday. If Mr Carrington never wanted to see me again, I couldn't wait a fortnight to find out, not when I was drowning in my feelings like this. I told myself I was mad to think of going round to see him, all the while knowing I would.

The day before we should have met I told Mum and Dad I was going for a walk, and took the bus to Mr Carrington's. My finger was hovering over the doorbell, when I realized this was the first time I'd ever visited his house except for a lesson. All my lines about passing by and just dropping in seemed ridiculous. But I'd come too far to turn round and go. So I sneaked down the path at the side of the house, thinking if only I could catch a glimpse of him, that might keep me going for another week.

I never planned to push open the unlocked French windows, or to walk through his sitting room, the first time I'd set foot there. I should have turned back when I heard sounds from the practice room. Someone was playing An Irish Jig from Tune-a-Day, and struggling. Still I walked on into the heart of the house. I stopped when I noticed the practice room door was half-open. If I flattened myself against the wall, I could see who was playing. It was a girl but, to my relief, she was only a baby, her hair, fair like mine, pulled into bunches. She wore a pink dress, with smocking across the chest and puffed sleeves. Scowling with concentration at the music stand, she stood with chubby calves apart, feet planted in strappy sandals.

All I had to do was cross to the other side of the door and Mr Carrington would be in my sightline. I moved as quickly as I could, praying he wouldn't look up. But I needn't have worried. There was no way he would have noticed me. He was staring at her, his eyes wide and pupils black, following every movement of the childish arms as they sawed to and fro. All the lines were smoothed from his face, as if the flesh had floated free of the bones. He looked as if he was dreaming while still awake.

Time to turn away. I walked down the checked tiles of the hall, knowing that never again would I feel the one loose tile wobble beneath my heel. Never again would the spotty mirror above the phone table hold my reflection as I ran my inquisitive hand over his mail. Sunlight streamed through the stained glass in the front door, shedding jewels of colour on the mat. These things were bits of the past now, and so was the burning look of want in Mr Carrington's eyes.

The End

The Jumper
ANDY FAWTHROP

Phil wasn't sure whether he felt sick or not. Occasional waves of nausea came over him, but just as quickly departed. However, he was absolutely certain of two things. Firstly he was now very sober and, secondly, it was a hell of a long way down. Not for the first time, he wished that he had not climbed over the railings and sat himself down with his legs dangling over the terrifying drop. He tried not to look down, but it was hard to avoid it, since it was the reason they were both here. He glanced nervously and carefully to his right, and looked at his companion.

The man beside him looked less nervous. In fact he seemed rather calm, perhaps resigned. Even though it was early evening now, he was dressed in what is known as full morning suit, including waistcoat, tails, collar, bow-tie and top hat. He had probably looked fairly smart earlier in the day, but at this later hour, he was undeniably the worse for wear. The collar was undone, the tie hung slackly about his neck. The sleeves of the jacket, and the trousers were marked with splashes of mud. The top-hat was slightly tilted to one side. He had obviously had a very long day.

He turned to Phil, and extended his hand to shake. 'Pleased to meet you, mate. My name's Don - Don Fiddler.'

Phil gripped the ledge with one hand and leaned back as far as he could. He extended his other hand gingerly and shook Don's hand. 'Phil Thomas.'
'This is very good of you, Phil. You don't have to do this, you know. But I do appreciate the gesture. Not many folks would do this. Most people would just walk past and leave me to it. In fact, to be honest, several already have.'

There was a short pause, and then he muttered 'Bastards!' very quietly under his breath.

Phil was surprised. 'You've been here a while then?'

'Hour or so, maybe longer,' conceded Don. 'I'm still thinking about it, you see.'

'About what?'

'Jumping of course! Why do you think I'm sitting here like this? It's not for the view.'

'Of course, of course,' said Phil soothingly. He thought that perhaps he ought to be getting on with the reason he was here - to talk this idiot out of jumping.

He had acted instinctively. He had been wandering home from the pub, after a rather long liquid lunch with the lads, when he'd spotted the figure of what turned out now to be Don. He'd felt quite merry, which was not surprising really. He'd been at that exact stage of drunkenness where one felt stupidly benevolent and well-inclined towards all men. He had immediately realised that what he was looking at was a soul in trouble, a fellow human being who needed his help. He had not stopped to think things through, he could admit that now, but had got himself over the railings before he knew what he was doing. The drop below him had served to sober him up within seconds. Now he could hardly back out. He couldn't get his mobile out of his pocket to phone the police, partly because he thought he might spook his new friend beside him, and partly because he was terrified of making any moves which might shift his own centre of gravity. If he was honest with himself he was actually terrified. He realised that he didn't want to be here, and yet now he was seated on the ledge next to a man who, in a rather different way, also did not want to be here.

'So what's it all about then?' he asked, indicating Don's outfit. 'Been to a wedding or something?'

Don's face darkened. 'I have, Phil, I have. That's exactly it. You've hit the nail right on the head there. Very astute of you. You are looking at a man who's been to a wedding. It was my wedding, actually.'

'Oh God!' thought Phil, but decided to say nothing.

'The last couple of weeks have just been a nightmare, what with one thing and another. It all started with Jessica - that's my intended - getting in a strop about the wedding arrangements. First it was about who was coming and who wasn't, then it was about who'd be sitting where at the reception afterwards. I didn't really care - it just seemed like trivial details to me. So I told her so. Big mistake. I said she ought to chill out a bit. That seemed to make things worse, rather than better. She said that I wasn't taking enough interest in the arrangements, and that she hoped it wasn't a sign of things to come. I asked her what she meant by that remark, and so she told me - at great length, I might add.'

Phil nodded sympathetically. 'I shouldn't worry about that, Don. I think it's a stage all women go through just before the wedding. It's just the stress. There's a lot of things to think about.'

'But that was just the start! She didn't speak to me for three days. Then when she finally did, it was "have you done this", and "have you done that?" I felt like a servant, not a groom-to-be.'

'Still...' began Phil, but Don cut across him.

'To say nothing of the fact that the usual womanly favours were withdrawn, if you understand my meaning?'

Phil nodded.

'We had a couple of blazing rows, and she was crying all the time. Then her mother started on me, asking me what I'd done to upset her darling Jessica. There was no arguing with her. She made sure I was firmly in the dog-house.' Don paused for breath and stared morosely down into the abyss for a moment. Phil was unsure what to say, but Don continued anyway. 'A week ago, the photographer rang up to cancel. Said he was emigrating. Left us in the lurch. So I had to chase round to book someone else at the last minute - which cost more, of course, because we were so desperate. I didn't tell Jessica. Thought it might upset her even more. I just paid the extra. Then three days ago the caterers rang to say that they couldn't do the reception after all - they'd just been closed down by the Public Health Department.' He sighed, and then groaned. 'You can't even begin to understand how difficult it is to find a company to cater for a wedding reception for 150 people at three days' notice. You wouldn't believe how many people I rang, nor how many of them just laughed at me and put the phone down. It was horrible, just horrible.' He put his head in his hands and groaned again.

Phil made a sympathetic noise, but was feeling distinctly deflated by this catalogue of woes. Still, he felt that he should be doing something to help. That's what he was here for, after all. Don seemed to be worse now than when he'd first joined him out on the ledge, which wasn't the idea at all. He cleared his throat.

'You've certainly had a rough time of it,' he began. 'I can see that. But you can't let these things get on top of you, you know. To every problem, there is a solution. You've got to think positive'. He smiled weakly, but encouragingly at Don.

Don failed to take the cue he was offered. Instead, he ran on with further woes. 'There's more yet - more you don't know about.'

'Is there?' asked Phil, fearing to hear more. He felt dreadful already. How much worse could it get?

'My parents arrived for the wedding yesterday. They didn't like the arrangements. They started questioning everything we'd already decided on. They think Jessica's not good enough for me, you see. I think they realised it was too late to stop things going ahead at this late stage, but they just wanted to cause as much trouble as possible. Then Jessica's father got wind of all this, and he decided to have it out with them. We all went out for a 'family' meal last night, and it all came to a head in the restaurant. He'd had a couple of drinks, and so had my dad, and they ended up having a huge row in public. Jessica ran out of the restaurant in tears, with her mother in pursuit. The meal was never eaten, but I still had to pick up the bill. It was a total disaster.'

Don sighed again, and looked off into the far distance, as if seeking inspiration. Phil was aware of people crossing the bridge behind them. A couple of pedestrians and quite a few cars had gone by in the past ten minutes. Nobody had seen fit to stop and wonder what was going on, to question why two men were sitting side by side on the other side of the safety barrier. He was desperate for someone to interrupt, to provide a distraction so that he might disentangle himself from this situation.

He had begun to feel quite deflated, hearing the turn that Don's story had taken. His earlier benevolent feelings, induced by drink, had evaporated completed. He had been reduced to a mood of maudlin pity. The poor, poor man, he thought. What a mess this all was. He didn't even feel convinced himself, but he felt he had to try at least.

'Look, Don, I know you've had a bad time and all that, but it's not worth killing yourself for. There's so much to live for. Why don't we both get back over the barrier? Let's go down to the pub and talk about it.'

'But we're already talking here,' Don said flatly.

'Well, yes, but if we went to the pub, I could buy you a drink. Then we could talk…er…more easily.'

'Besides, you haven't heard the rest of it yet.'

'There's more?' asked Phil. What else could there be? How much worse could it get?

'Oh yes. I thought everything had calmed down by this morning. We'd all had a night's sleep, and I hoped everybody had had time to think things over. Apart from the threatening phone call from Jessica's father, just to remind me that if I let down his little girl, he'd personally tear me limb from limb, nothing much happened this morning. I got dressed and got myself to the church on time. The congregation turned up. The vicar turned up. The Best Man didn't lose the ring. Everything was in place. The only snag was that Jessica decided not to come. After we'd been waiting half an hour, just her sister turned up on her own. She brought a note from Jessica.'

'Oh God!' said Phil. 'That's really awful! You poor bloke!'

Don was right to be sitting here after all. No wonder he wanted to kill himself. What was there to live for?

'She said that she'd realised over the last two weeks just what a pig I was. That I wasn't the man for her. That she couldn't marry me because we wouldn't be happy together. That the wedding was off. She jilted me in front of all those people!' He sighed again, and paused for effect.

Phil now knew what he had to do. Carefully he pulled himself upright, clinging to the barrier, then began to climb over back to safety.

Don looked up at him in panic. 'What are you doing? Where are you going? Aren't you going to help me? Talk me out of it?'

'I'd like to, Don, but that's the worst story I've ever heard. If I sit here any longer one of us is bound to jump, and I've decided it's not going to be me. I'm afraid you'll have to make your own mind up.'

'Thanks,' muttered Don. 'You've been a great help.'

The End.